PRAISE F

"I could not help but feel the pain, the anticipation, and the heartaches of this family as I read the book *By Your Side*. I was not able to stop reading it until I was finished, and deep compassion for this family emerged for all they have been through. Misty is a beautiful author and it was an honor to read her story and the story of Stephanie, to see the world through someone else's eyes and read the details of what life must have been like going through their tragedy opened my heart. Sometimes we cannot find meaning, justice, or a silver lining in certain experiences, and yet Misty has taken the tragedy of her sister's disappearance and weaved hope and a divine thread of spirit into it. I could not help but feel like her sister would be extremely proud to have a voice through the sister that is still here to honor her journey. I highly recommend this book, tears will flow, but your heart will also open."

—**Melissa Kim Corter,** artist and intuitive guide. Author of *Nudges from Your Spirit* and *Seasons of Change*

"*By Your Side: A Journey of Two Sisters through Love and Sacrifice* is a true and relatable story of heartbreak and heart expansion. Misty Thompson weaves you through a web of fear, grief, and sadness and brings you to the other side.... to love, awareness and appreciation. Misty's journey with her sister and her experience of unconditional love will bring you a greater understanding of your connection to the Spirit world... and your ability to open your heart even more."

—**Sunny Dawn Johnston,** best-selling author of *Invoking the Archangels*, *The Love Never Ends* and *365 Days of Angel Prayers*

"Misty Thompson has opened the doors to the past to relive her sister's journey through life and death in this tale of two sisters who were separated too soon in the physical world, yet their bond strengthens more and more as time passes by, ultimately leading the author on a spiritual journey to discover her own unique gifts and find her true calling.

"It's not every day you get to hear from someone who personally has lived through hell. Misty Thompsons book was real, raw and a true testament to how spirit works even in the most horrific situations.

"This book will not only give you pause to feeling gratitude for your loved ones currently in your life but it will also open your eyes to a new perspective on how to walk through tragedy with grace and continue to shine your light into the world. A beautiful read that I could not put down."

—**Jodie Harvala,** psychic medium, author of *The ABC's of Intuition* and *The Magic of Space Clearing.* Creator of Spirit School

"Misty set out to honor her sister's unsolved murder through this mystery set in a small Arizona town, but through this story we discover the two sisters are now closer than ever, and she truly believes Stephanie is still with her and even helped her find the answers the family were seeking for far too long.

"This book is gripping and heartfelt, and it urged me to take a look at my own relationships with loved once and to cherish those still with me, but it also offers hope that even those who depart from the physical world are also still there ... and always *By Your Side."*

—**Shanda Trofe,** publisher & author coach, bestselling author of *Write from the Heart* and *Authorpreneur*

By Your Side

A Journey of Two Sisters through Love and Sacrifice

MISTY PROFFITT-THOMPSON

BY YOUR SIDE

A Journey of Two Sisters through Love and Sacrifice

By Misty Proffitt-Thompson

Copyright © 2017. Misty Proffitt-Thompson. All rights reserved. No part of this publication may be reproduced, distributed, or transmitted in any form or by any means, including photocopying, recording, or other electronic or mechanical methods, without the prior written permission of the publisher, except in the case of brief quotations embodied in critical reviews and certain other noncommercial uses permitted by copyright law.

Transcendent Publishing
PO Box 66202
St. Pete Beach, FL 33736
www.TranscendentPublishing.com

ISBN-10: 0-9987576-6-7
ISBN-13: 978-0-9987576-6-7
Library of Congress Control Number: 2017939593

Printed in the United States of America.

This work depicts actual events in the life of the author as truthfully as recollection permits and/or can be verified by research. Occasionally, dialogue consistent with the character or nature of the person speaking has been supplemented. All persons within are actual individuals; there are no composite characters. The names of some individuals have been changed to respect their privacy. Although the author and publisher have made every effort to ensure that the information in this book was correct at press time, the author and publisher do not assume and hereby disclaim any liability to any party for any loss, damage, or disruption caused by errors or omissions, whether such errors or omissions result from negligence, accident, or any other cause.

DEDICATION

This book is dedicated to my sister, Stephanie. I am sorry for the way your life ended; however, I know there is a plan for us. Thank you for watching over me and my family. I appreciate your encouragement while I wrote this book, as it was difficult to re-live these emotions. I know that others will be touched because so many have had a loved one who has passed tragically. There is so much guilt, shame, and regret for us who are still living that we must work through. I know that you are proud of me and even though our physical life together was a bit chaotic, our spiritual life is one of peace and love. Thank you for helping me with my life lessons.

ACKNOWLEDGEMENTS

I would like to acknowledge the following people:

My family, Tom, Brittany, Jacob, Joshua, and Tuesday. You all have been and always will be my greatest teachers in life. You each are here for me in a different way and I love you all! I am completely grateful for each and every one of you.

To my grandkids, Josiah, Damian, Ashton, and Caleb, you are so much fun to be around and I love you all tremensdously.

To my mentors, Sunny, Shanda, Melissa, and Jodie: You all have supported me in different ways and encouraged me to be my true self.

Thank you!

CONTENTS

PROLOGUE: Finding Light in Tragedy i

CHAPTER ONE: Stephanie is Missing 1

CHAPTER TWO: Sisters Growing Up Together 9

CHAPTER THREE: The Beginning of the End 25

CHAPTER FOUR: The Craziness Starts 33

CHAPTER FIVE: Stephanie Makes Her Presence Known 39

CHAPTER SIX: Going Nowhere 49

CHAPTER SEVEN: Saying Goodbye 79

CHAPTER EIGHT: Believing the Unbelievable 95

CHAPTER NINE: Focusing on My Gifts 113

CHAPTER TEN: My Life is Changing 119

EPILOGUE: By Your Side 125

MEMORIES 127

ABOUT THE AUTHOR 137

PROLOGUE
Finding Light in Tragedy

Is it possible to be closer to someone after they have passed from this world? My sister Stephanie and I weren't close growing up; in fact, we fought more often than we got along. I can only imagine how exasperated mom was having to deal with us. We were 18 months apart and even though we didn't look alike, we were mistaken for twins. We could have been because mom dressed us alike.

My sister passed away over 20 years ago, and although it seems like yesterday, it was a lifetime ago. Her death was a bewildering tragedy with many unanswered questions. I have come to accept that we will never know all the answers, but I also have peace in that acceptance. I sometimes wonder what our lives would be like if she were still alive. I envision our days spent in celebration of each other's accomplishments, and sharing each other's sorrows. The time since her death, now longer than her time spent on earth, is difficult to fathom.

I live in a small, rural Arizona town near the New Mexico border, and this is where Stephanie died. We lived in other states when growing up, with bigger cities where tragedy was routine, but not here, in our hometown.

I am now 47 years old and a retired Federal Law

Enforcement Officer. When she passed, I was so naïve, being only 24 years old and just starting my career. Three of my four children were under the age of seven and I was married to my first husband, Roger.

It feels like a piece of me is missing with her not here. I divorced Roger and am now married to Thomas. We have a daughter who is a freshman in high school. My three older children are living on their own and they all have young children. I believe that Stephanie knows of my grandchildren but it would be nice if she was here with us physically. Stephanie wasn't able to have children, so I believe she appreciates my children and their children. I'm certain that they would have loved her as well. I can just visualize Stephanie at an awards night assembly with all of us. She is present in spirit now, and our encounters with her are teaching my children and grandchildren that those who die are with us still.

Many of you can understand the challenges I have experienced. The circumstances may be different but the pain is the same, regardless of how your loved ones passed. I am still grieving after all this time due to the mysteries surrounding her death. She is better off where she is, but to think that someone murdered her leaves me sickened.

Our local Sheriff's Office mishandled the investigation. Some members of the Sheriff's Office treated my family as if we were the guilty ones. The Sheriff seemed to think he was doing us a favor by looking for her. I have contacted the Sheriff's Office recently and learned they have new staff members. I wish these officers could have conducted the investigation back in the early 90s. I believe they would have been more responsible and professional. At the same time, through Stephanie's sacrifice, I have come to know more about spirit and my life path.

I should not have been surprised that she died tragically like she did, knowing her lifestyle, yet I was. At the time, I wasn't able to relate to how she chose to live her short life and I don't know if I ever will. I just have to believe that we are all on the path of our choosing, and that everything happens for a reason. We are here to learn from the events of our lives. Otherwise, what would be the point? Despite my great loss, this experience has changed me for the better. I am now in touch with my spiritual gifts and realize that our time in this physical realm is short. We are meant to live life to the fullest. Whether I am enjoying a quick trip to the ocean to cleanse my soul, attending a spiritual workshop to infuse positive energy into my mind and body, or binge-watching television while curled up in my warm, comfortable bed, life is brief. We are here to grow and make the most of the love and joy we find.

I have healed from the grief of my sister's death, and been guided to tell Stephanie's story as well as mine. This process has been therapeutic and transformational. I am convinced that it is my intended spiritual journey. Many people have experienced a similar tragedy. I hope by telling our story you will find peace, forgiveness and hope.

This book is written to honor her life and to express my gratitude for her guidance in my life. When she transitioned, the need to help each other became essential. She needed me to help her on the other side. At the same time, I needed her to help me on earth. Helping her and following my path is the way I find light in tragedy...

MISTY PROFFITT-THOMPSON

CHAPTER ONE
Stephanie is Missing

"Stephanie is missing!" My mom's voice broke and she sounded frantic. It was Wednesday, August 18, 1993. "Something terrible has happened to her, I just know it."

I couldn't help but be skeptical. I had heard this many times before. My sister's lifestyle was much different than mine. She abused drugs and had done so for most of her teenage/adult life. When she was high, she was unreliable, irresponsible, selfish, and manipulative, but when she was sober, she was kind, nurturing, helpful, generous, and funny.

During the destructive periods, I could see through her schemes to manipulate mom and dad. Most of the time she was after money so she could buy drugs. Stephanie struggled with her inadequacies and her need for attention, but that just made her human, and we all have our vices. If Stephanie wasn't asking my parents for money, she was getting attention and money for her habit from strangers.

Ultimately, she made decisions that resulted in her death. I take comfort in believing that our choices come with a lesson, and Stephanie now has the benefit of all her life lessons.

Andrew Goodman, my sister's ex-husband, called mom at 12:30 p.m. that afternoon with his explanation of what happened to Stephanie. Mom was curious what his story would be, since he was insisting that she report Stephanie missing to the local Sheriff's Office.

The concern was that Stephanie would miss her scheduled court date of August 23 on charges filed against her the previous month. It was assumed her disappearance was an effort to avoid her court hearing.

Stephanie had stolen personal checks from her ex-boyfriend, Raymond, forged his name, and cashed the checks. She was charged with stealing and forging checks in excess of $2,000.00. Stephanie was ordered to be held in the Graham County Jail but was released on her own recognizance. She was to check-in with mom daily.

August 18th ended with no word from her, and before that date, she had called every day. Mom talked to both of us daily. I still wasn't convinced that something was wrong. I did, however, know that mom feared these claims were real.

Because the Sheriff's Office was not concerned about her disappearance and would not act until she had been gone for 24 hours, Mom and Andrew went to the Sheriff's Office to report her missing on August 19, 1993.

Stephanie was well known to the Sheriff's Office because of her lifestyle and associates, and Andrew was no exception. He was an informant for the Sheriff's Office. He would set up drug deals and then notify the Officers once the transactions were complete. He had several run-ins with law enforcement through the years. Most of those involved beating his female companions, and unfortunately, this included my sister.

At the Sheriff's Office, mom and Andrew gave their statement for the initial report. "I was the last person to see her [Stephanie] alive," Andrew reported.

This disturbed me as this meant that he was with her when she died.

Based on his actions, it seemed that Andrew didn't try to help Stephanie. Andrew continued, "It was 3:30 in the morning on August 18th and me and Stephanie was arguing about her drinking around the house."

This was an ongoing disagreement, and they had argued off and on for the last couple of days prior to the 18th.

"At about midnight, Stephanie insisted that I wake up. I finally got up after she kept pestering me. I opened my eyes and she said she wanted to go out. She WOULD NOT stop bothering me."

He said he grabbed a pair of pants stained with oil and a ripped shirt on the floor, then dressed. He put on tennis shoes after dumping out sand from the desert.

They decided to drive out to the hot tubs on Tanque Road. When they stopped for something to drink, she bought herself a Gatorade and an orange juice for him. They then drove east of town to Heckle Road to get to the Tanque hot tubs.

I never did understand why they went to the convenience store that was 20 miles in the opposite direction. There were at least two other stores they would have passed on their route. The Sheriff's Office did not seem concerned with this discrepancy.

The problems started when the lights on his vehicle failed three miles out on the desert road.

He claimed, "I pulled the vehicle over and tried to figure out what was wrong and we started arguing again. Stephanie opened the door and slammed it behind her. She sat down on the side of the road and I tried to convince her to get back in the vehicle, but her stubborn side came out and she refused. I left her on the side of that dirt road."

He pulled over once again and tried to repair the lights a second time, but was unsuccessful.

He turned the vehicle around to head back to the drop-off point. He thought she'd cool down out there alone in the dark.

It would have been hot even at that time of morning, and she would have been exposed to the elements.

Once he returned, she was still there, so he tried to convince her to get back into the vehicle but she again refused.

Andrew continued, "Since my lights weren't working, I decided to drive back to my house, pick up my van, and go back to get her. That was always my intention."

Driving back to his house would have taken time, especially when driving at night with only his parking lights. He estimated that it would take an hour to an hour and a half to return to where he left her. When he went back to pick her up, she was gone.

I couldn't help but wonder why someone in their right mind would leave her out there. There were many other options available to him, yet he abandoned her and then lost her. Maybe he too had been drinking or doing drugs.

Common sense says that he was either lying and they never drove out there or he purposely left her there to die. That meant that my sister would never be seen alive again. We will never know why he made the choices he did and because of his poor judgment, our family will always be haunted by her loss.

He thought that maybe she could walk the seven-mile journey to town and possibly find a house and use their phone or find a pay phone to call Raymond. For someone in her condition to walk seven miles seemed absurd. For her to call Raymond was the one part of his story that was believable.

She would pit the two of them against each other and since Andrew and she were fighting, that idea seemed plausible, but the odds of her finding a phone to call Raymond in the early morning hours were slim to none. She was not in the best of shape, she smoked, didn't have a healthy diet, recently broke her foot, and was a drug user off and on. How would she be able to make it down a three-mile stretch of dirt road and then walk another four miles on a highway to the nearest phone?

The Sheriff's Deputy said he would contact Raymond to ask if he had seen Stephanie.

The Deputy asked Andrew again how many miles he had gone on Heckle Road before Stephanie exited the vehicle. When he left her, Andrew said he checked the odometer reading so he would know where to look once he returned. His odometer showed 3.7 miles.

He stated that he also looked at his watch because he wanted to calculate the time it would take for her to walk to the highway from the Gatorade bottle he left as a marker. It would make more sense if he said he left the drink for her.

As Stephanie sat on the side of that dark desert road, did he leave knowing she would be forever lost?

When Stephanie wasn't heard from on that critical day, mom decided to search for Stephanie.

The Sheriff's Office was notified the day of her disappearance, but because she hadn't been gone for 24 hours, they didn't take mom's statement until the 19th.

With the August temperatures in the 100's, mom went out to the desert to look for her daughter. She walked through what I call scrub land, a rocky area with mesquite trees and cactus. The Gila Monsters, scorpions, and rattlesnakes in the desert proved her dedication to her daughter.

The Deputy drove to Raymond's residence on the 19th and did not find Stephanie. Raymond said she was with Andrew as they passed by his residence. That was about 10:30 am on August 18th, another discrepancy. Based on Andrew's statements to the Sheriff's Deputy, Stephanie was already missing.

The official search for Stephanie started on August 19th. The Search and Rescue team assembled and the area mom searched was searched again. Shoe prints consistent with the type and size of footwear Andrew said she was wearing were found in the dirt. They were followed a short distance but the tracks ended.

No pictures were taken nor was a print cast taken. Ultimately a 300-foot radius was covered with negative results.

For the next 55 days, we didn't know whether she would walk in the door with no memory of the last seven-plus weeks, or her body would be found in the desert. We didn't know what was ahead for us. It was better that I didn't know. I had to take everything coming at me in small doses, that way it wasn't such a shock.

In the days to come, I would become less trusting of the people in my community, local law enforcement, my co-workers, and my family. I learned how judgmental strangers in town could be about my sister. Some were kind and wanted to help. Some were harsh in their statements about her lifestyle. The local law enforcement in town was involved in corruption, deceit, and bribery. This wasn't true of all the officers; however, many in leadership roles were dishonest. My co-workers were supportive with the exception of a few gossips. Even some in my family were judgmental and I dealt with that as best I could.

CHAPTER TWO
Sisters Growing Up Together

I was born in the month of February, 1969, and Stephanie followed in August, 1970. We were what I thought was a normal family. Looking back, I can see the dysfunction, and it spiraled out of control as we got older. Mom and dad met at a party in 1968 and although dad was married, they had a one-night stand. I'm sure they weren't expecting to see each other again, but mom became pregnant with me, and back then the honorable thing was for my dad to divorce his wife and marry mom. They were married in October 1968 in Las Vegas. By the end of 1970, it was the four of us.

My earliest childhood memory was when I was about four years old. We lived in a modest three-bedroom, two-bathroom house in Tempe, Arizona. It was a pleasant neighborhood. Down the street was a park where dad took my sister and me to play. I was excited about living where we did, not only because of the park, but because we were just a few blocks away from Ladmo. In Arizona during the '70s and '80s, Wallace and Ladmo were hosts of a televised kid's program that aired every weekday. They were Arizona television royalty. I realized later that I could have been told Ladmo was our neighbor just to get me to behave.

Little did I know back then that we were far from normal. It was the early 1970s and mom and dad hosted hippie parties at the house. We had a formal living room where dad kept our stereo system, with a record player and 8-track player. This sound system was stored on a shelf held up by cement bricks spray-painted gold. A green shag carpet ran throughout the house with a black light on for the parties.

Our 8-track player would rock to Three Dog Night, Elton John, Carole King, The Steve Miller Band and other rock classics. I even had my own favorites. I would sing my lungs out to my 8-track of Donny and Marie Osmond's, *I'm Leaving It All Up To You.*

I don't remember if my dad was working then. I do remember mom working nights and when she was gone, dad had his own parties. He probably didn't party every night, but that's what I remember most about living in that house.

Stephanie thought it was fun because we would dress up as waitresses and serve refreshments to the guests. When it got crazy, dad would send us to bed. To make sure we slept, he gave us Nyquil. That always did the trick.

I started kindergarten at that time and always followed the rules, while Stephanie was the rebel. I remember when Stephanie and I were told to keep pink foam rollers in our hair all night. I left mine in, even though it was uncomfortable, but Stephanie tore them all out. We have pictures of us the next day, standing in our nice dresses with Stephanie's hair flat and mine curly.

I was also told not to get into a car with anyone other than my parents. A close friend of mom and dad's came to pick me up from school and I refused to get into the car. I knew him and loved sitting on his lap when he would visit. He had been a friend of the family for years, but I followed my parents' directions.

If I was told to do something, most of the time I obeyed. The exception was when I wanted candy from the store. If I didn't get it, I would throw temper tantrums. These were brutal fits. I would throw myself down while kicking and screaming. The worst part was when I'd bang my head on the walls. I am not proud of my behavior, but I was a five-year-old.

Stephanie, on the other hand, was the opposite. She didn't throw temper tantrums, she just did what she wanted. She would cut up her socks because they were rough on her skin, and she would curse at my dad when he teased her. I would never, ever use a curse word at that age. Even to this day, I won't.

Life was simpler in the 1970s and most people could be trusted, although today it's much different. Stephanie and I had fun together, despite our differences. And as much as we fought, if anyone bullied me, she would come to my defense. We were best friends and loved each other.

We often visited our next-door neighbor. She was married and must have been in her 50s. She played hide-and-seek with us. Her house had an awful smell, like a day care for the elderly. That medicinal scent mixed with the odor of death.

While there, I always wondered why she'd disappear. I once saw her in the kitchen drinking what I thought was dark apple juice. I realize now that it was whiskey. Her eyes were always puffy and bloodshot, her face was red and she had a peculiar smell. I didn't recognize it then but I do now, alcohol, coming from her sweat and breath. That explains how she could tolerate us for hours.

Stephanie had to undergo surgery on her eyes. She was cross-eyed and after the surgery had to wear a patch. I was sad that she had to suffer through this. Once the patch came off, her eyes were no longer crossed and I was grateful she had her sight corrected. I didn't know at the time that I am empathetic. I seem to experience others' emotions, and if a tragedy occurs, I feel their pain and sadness.

Most days I would hear my parents yelling at each other and not know why they were arguing. I would stay in the bedroom with Stephanie and we distracted ourselves by playing until it was over. Sometimes mom would bring us into her bedroom and lock the three of us in. I remember dad banging on the door and demanding we open it. I would fall asleep on mom's bed and stay there until the next morning. If he'd wanted, he could have broken down the flimsy pressed-wood door.

One night mom came home from work and could see smoke circling the family room and hear laughter. The pungent odor told her it was marijuana. She was incredulous that dad would do that with us in the house. Again, the screaming started and Stephanie and I were sent to mom's room for the night.

Before I began first grade, we moved to another residence in Tempe, Arizona. It was a small two-bedroom trailer. By now Stephanie had started school, and she was even more rebellious.

One day, Stephanie wanted us to collect money from the neighbors. Being an honest kid, I didn't like the idea.

Stephanie told me to say it was money for the poor, and since we were poor we would keep it. It made perfect sense. She was always the leader and I the follower.

The next year we moved to a two-bedroom apartment in Tempe. During this time, we used food stamps. At the store, we loaded the cart with junk food. My diet consisted of Fritos and bean dip, soda and ice cream. I do not remember apples, bananas, salad, or anything healthy, but I was a kid and I loved it.

When mom and dad got into a big fight mom sometimes took us to the rural town where I currently live. Mom, Stephanie, and I stayed with my granny or in a small apartment. My dad would drive up and visit us and I always felt sorry for him. Mom and granny would talk bad about him and Stephanie would join in, while I was just sad. Mom would go back to my dad and the dysfunction would continue. They would fight, we would drive to granny's, then we'd go back to dad again.

I didn't understand all that back and forth and didn't like it. If mom didn't want to be with dad, why did she return to him.

He had a temper and although I do not recall him ever hitting us, I know he came close to it.

When we'd leave him, I imagined my dad as being unhappy. He was probably having the time of his life, with no kids to bother him and no responsibilities. My heart would ache for him and I was often depressed.

I can see now that mom was desperate to make dad happy. She always had dinner on the table, bought us decent clothes, and our house was always clean. She would make him lunch every morning on the rare occasions when he worked.

My dad is sorry now for the way he treated mom, but back then, he was selfish. He did the best he could and that is all we can ask of anybody. Stephanie would grow up to display the same qualities dad had.

When I was about seven and we were living in Tempe with my dad, granny came to visit us. Mom, granny, Stephanie and I were in our car when once again mom and granny were criticizing my dad. Again, Stephanie joined in and I remember clutching my blanket as tears ran down my face.

When we pulled up in front of an apartment complex, mom slammed the car in park, opened the door and began screaming. I saw my dad with his arm around a woman's waist going into one of the apartments.

I was devastated. First, mom and granny were trashing my dad. Then, my dad had his arm around someone who wasn't my mom.

But now, I don't judge them. They did the best they could at the time. I am sure they would do things differently if that could have changed the outcome of Stephanie's life. It is painful knowing my parents blame themselves, especially when I believe that she is okay. Life is a series of lessons and mom and dad must accept and forgive themselves.

It wasn't always sad when we were young. We enjoyed performing dance routines we choreographed for mom and dad. We also took walks in the park as a family and occasionally went to movie theaters.

I remember seeing *Star Wars*, the original, and *A Star is Born*, with Barbra Streisand and Kris Kristofferson. That bad boy image portrayed in the movie reminded me of dad. I watch those movies today and they take me back to the good times when we were happy together.

As Stephanie and I got older, we grew to hate one another and would physically fight. It was astonishing how opposite we became. I got good grades while hers were average, she was outgoing and I was shy, she was brave and I was afraid, and I wanted to please while she wanted to shock.

When I was about eight we all moved from Arizona to Long Beach, California. Again, the dysfunction continued but it was no longer easy to run to Safford; it is a nine-hour drive instead of a four-hour drive.

Mom seemed weary and just plain exhausted. All her time and energy was spent on us. She would do without so that Stephanie and I had everything.

As I got older, I became skeptical. When my parents fought, I wasn't sure it was serious. I had seen the pattern before and we always went back to dad.

We finally returned to Arizona and lived with granny, her husband (my step-grandfather), my aunt and my uncle. Seven people living in a small two-bedroom trailer. Mom worked two jobs to save money and get our own place. I am sure she was desperate for us to live on our own.

During this time Stephanie was molested. I remember we were helping an older man with his yardwork. For some reason, I had to leave while Stephanie stayed. The next thing I remember was granny waving a gun, threatening to kill the man who touched Stephanie. Mom was running after her trying to calm her down. That was one of the scariest moments in my life.

At ten years old, I didn't understand what being molested meant. Later, I believed if I hadn't left she would not have been abused.

Stephanie's childhood may have contributed to her lifestyle as an adult, including this molestation.

Again, when I found out what happened I felt horrible. I tortured myself, asking why I didn't stay longer. I finally learned that we each have a life journey for our souls to learn lessons. With that awareness, I let go of the guilt. If he wanted to molest her, he would have done so whether I was there or not.

We all have free will and make our own decisions. Stephanie also had the choice not to let that experience define her. She could have forgiven herself and realized that it wasn't her fault. She could have made that awful experience a lesson in forgiveness, not only for the man who did that to her but also for herself. I am at peace knowing that as a ten-year-old child, I couldn't prevent that from happening.

Tragedy is inevitable, but if we don't heal from it, we self-medicate. It could be by overeating, doing drugs, or drinking alcohol, but the result is that we destroy ourselves.

Mom and dad divorced in 1979. In 1980, mom remarried and at first it wasn't bad, except when my step-dad would drink and say hateful things to mom, Stephanie and me.

My step-dad also instigated fights between me and my step-brother. I am not a fighter, but when my step-dad would tell my step-brother that he needed to kick my ass, I learned to fight and quick. Mom let it happen. Feeling betrayed by my mom was the worst part.

When it rained he'd come home drunk. He was a construction worker and those rainy days meant no work. My step-dad would fight with mom for no reason other than he was drunk.

When Stephanie was in sixth grade and I was in seventh, we moved to West Phoenix and started attending Desert Horizon Elementary School. Our living conditions were better but I would often be annoyed with mom. In hindsight, I could have been kinder, but teenagers aren't always nice to their parents.

When mom shared stories from her youth, I realized what I thought was normal was wealthy for her. I began learning about gratitude back then. We lived in a three-bedroom house and mom did her best to have food in the house. She cooked dinner every night even though she worked a 9-to-5 job. I was embarrassed to bring friends over and told her we should have a better house, a better car, and better furniture. We had two couches that didn't match, an oddball chair, and a kitchen bench made by my step-dad. It was functional, but not good enough for me.

My two step-brothers were a nightmare. One step-brother was the oldest, then me, then Stephanie, then my younger step-brother.

My oldest step-brother was autistic and required constant supervision. When mom wasn't working, she was either cleaning and cooking or she was helping him. Stephanie was patient with him but I didn't like his outbursts. I liked playing with him when we were younger, but as he got older he became violent, so I avoided him.

My step-dad was often drunk, so mom helped my step-brother with homework from his special-needs school.

Mom couldn't focus on us because her time went to him. Looking back, I think Stephanie needed that attention.

Stephanie was pushing the boundaries and was beginning to spiral out of control with mom and our step-dad. She was ditching school, getting bad grades, hanging out with older boys, and smoking cigarettes. Crazy behavior for a 12-year-old. For me, that was unacceptable. I knew that led to destruction.

I watched my parents and learned from them. My parents did not finish high school and they struggled financially. I decided to go to college and have a career. I wanted to live comfortably, not paycheck-to-paycheck.

Stephanie made a friend in her class and because mom and my step-dad befriended the girl's mother, we often went to her house for dinner. When we were there, I felt uncomfortable. I didn't know yet that I was picking up on negative emotions, and couldn't shield myself. I didn't know why I felt like something was wrong.

Once when we were there I realized what was wrong; my parents and the girl's mom were smoking marijuana. Stephanie was smug and arrogant. She made me feel like I didn't belong. This was another sign that I would have a different life than that of my family's.

I did not think like them and they could not understand me. I didn't feel right when my parents were breaking the law by smoking marijuana. It seemed bizarre that they were smoking with us there. Mom used to shield Stephanie and me from dad getting high with his friends. She'd get so angry, but now was doing it herself.

During those pre-teen/teenage years, Stephanie preyed on me, her goody-two-shoes victim. Teenage life is tough, but when your sister leads the pack, it's unbearable. I have now learned that it is how I react that matters, not what is done to me.

Back then, I would get furious with her. Mom used to say that she was jealous of me but I couldn't understand why. I loved my sister, but she knew how to push my buttons.

During my teenage years, she knew I had a crush on a guy who was a year or two older than me. I was excited when he asked me to go see a movie. Most of the girls in our neighborhood liked him. He was polite to all of us, and a gentleman. He had talent in freehand drawing and drew pictures for me.

Stephanie did whatever she could to keep me away from him. The day I was supposed to meet him at the local theater to see the movie, *Friday the 13th*, she sabotaged me. After I left the house, she called him and said I couldn't go, and as a result he stayed home. I went to the theater and when he wasn't there, I went inside thinking he was already seated. I was devastated when I thought I had been stood up. I started crying right there in the theater. I felt so humiliated and stupid, a 13-year-old at the movies by herself.

When I got home she was gloating over what she'd done. She'd told him that I was a prude and wouldn't let him kiss my cheek or even hold my hand. I considered those to be innocent, but it was none of her business. It didn't matter anyway, because her ultimate betrayal was to have sex with him.

I am not sure that story was true but the more I thought about it, the more I realized it probably was. I remember a poster I saw in a friend's room around that time. A beautiful Monarch butterfly, orange and black, with the phrase, "If you love something set it free. If it comes back to you it's yours, if it doesn't it was never meant to be."

I certainly did not love him, but I did have a major crush. I remembered the words on that poster and decided to not dwell on it. I held my head high knowing I did nothing wrong. I eventually started dating someone else and my infatuation became a distant memory.

Her next idea was to run away with three 16-year-olds. 'Run away' is too dramatic; they went joy-riding. One of the boys' parents owned a trans-am and the group decided that it would be fun to "borrow" the car and drive it to where our dad lived, in Long Beach, California. The idea sounds ridiculous now. I don't know how they navigated LA freeways. We didn't have cell phones, no GPS, only paper maps. Mom and my step-dad considered this unacceptable behavior. In Stephanie's eyes, she wasn't running away, she just wanted to see her father.

She ended up staying in California with him for a few weeks while mom organized her living arrangements, and later she returned to us. She was surprised to find out that instead of staying with us she was admitted to St. Luke's Hospital in Phoenix. It was a program for unruly teens.

The day she was admitted was scary for me so I cannot imagine what her feelings were. No one wanted to be locked up there, although those girls had reasons to be there. Deep down I knew my sister was a good person and I am sure those other girls were, too. All she wanted was attention and love. Maybe she didn't feel worthy of having a healthy relationship. She had done some wild things but I wanted mom to give her another chance, knowing my sister wouldn't obey. I just felt sorry for her.

I vowed never to be forced into a place like that. Everything was earned and considered a privilege. The use of the phone, watching television, make-up, curling irons, blow dryers, and visitors, all were based on good behavior. If anyone misbehaved, they would have to sit in a small space in the main room and not move or speak.

On the way home, mom was quiet and I stared out the window, lost in thought. I wondered what Stephanie was doing. I saw the worry on mom's face, and felt her pain. I was sad for her and wished I could lift her burden.

I couldn't understand how this happened. All I wanted was for us to be a normal family. Little did I know that "normal" doesn't exist.

I had a vision of living in a three- to four-bedroom house with upscale furniture. Instead of an older car with the seats ripped, I wanted us to have a newer car that was stylish.

Most of the time I was annoyed with Stephanie but I still loved her. She was funny, caring, protective and good-hearted.

Once her stay in the hospital ended, she went to live with dad. Stephanie's move to another state must have been frightening for mom, but it was a relief for us all.

Stephanie could go to a home that was financially stable. Dad was doing well at his job and could provide her with the luxuries I never had. Stephanie attended private schools, wore expensive clothes and was spoiled. That was the life I wanted and I was jealous. I was the one with good behavior, but continued to live in her shadow. While she was gone, I didn't reach out to her, and we had no contact.

A few summers later, I went to California to visit my dad and she was no longer living there. It turns out that she left everything that was handed to her to live on the streets. She had met a guy who introduced her to drugs. My dad couldn't control her behavior. Stephanie was her father's daughter, so maybe he understood her more than the rest of us did.

I couldn't understand her attraction to some drugged-out stranger living on the streets of Long Beach in the early 1980s.

I became close friends with two of her schoolmates and would sometimes hang out with Stephanie. Southern California was a dream come true for me because we would spend all day at Seal Beach, flirt with surfer boys, and shop at the Lakewood Mall or the new Long Beach Mall. When we were bored, we would drive to Disneyland only 20 minutes away.

When summer ended, I stayed with my dad. Except by now, he had lost his job. For me there was no private school, no fancy clothes, and no money. We lived on food stamps and unemployment checks. I balanced the checkbook and paid the bills. I ran the household and his job was to sign the checks. It was embarrassing and hard, but I learned responsibility.

When I lived with my dad, my sister would visit the neighborhood but ignore me. It was common for her to break into our house while I was in school and my dad was at job interviews. She would steal my dad's credit cards, cash, anything of value. More than once she stole my cassette tapes, boom box, and clothing. Music was my only indulgence and she stole it. The worst part was that she would flaunt what she'd sold for drugs. She had no remorse. It hurt that my possessions were taken, but it hurt more knowing that my own sister robbed me. I was heartbroken.

Helping Stephanie was a priority for my family and a constant battle. She ended up back in Arizona with mom when she was fifteen. Mom moved to the little town where I now live and Stephanie enrolled in high school but found it impossible after living with so much freedom. Being on a "normal" schedule set her up for failure. She was used to doing whatever she pleased whenever she wanted, and she was behind in her classes. She ended up dropping out and getting her GED.

I stayed with my dad for one year and then moved back to mom's in Arizona. I was able to adapt to life in a small town. In my junior year, I had my beautiful daughter. Stephanie was also living in this town and trying to find her way.

I graduated from Safford High School in 1987, and while my plans were set, she was constantly changing hers. She would try to do what was expected of her, and then would go back to the streets. Maybe she thought my life was harsh, working to support myself and my children. She made friends with values like hers and spiraled down into the same destructive lifestyle of drug abuse.

Stephanie married her first husband in 1987 and began making better choices. She was trying to get pregnant but wasn't successful, although she did have a tubal pregnancy, and then was told she could not have children. That was heartbreaking for her. She started spending time with my oldest daughter, who was one year old. She loved her niece and was a help to me. Her marriage didn't last and I didn't ask why. He is now remarried and has a family.

When she wasn't using, Stephanie was compassionate, easygoing and reliable. But those old habits called to her. Soon she was back on drugs. My daughter didn't understand why those visits with Aunt Stephanie came to an end. I knew when Stephanie was lying to me or when she was high. I guess it was because I had witnessed her years of addiction. I decided to cut off all communication and keep my family away from her.

I now know that everyone must follow their own path. A direction that is right for me may not be right for others. Stephanie chose her life. She made choices and accepted the results. You must admit, that is admirable. Some of us are not strong enough to follow our heart, but I believe Stephanie did.

CHAPTER THREE
The Beginning of the End

I am not sure when Stephanie met Andrew, but they were married in April, 1990. Stephanie knew she should divorce him, but it took her two attempts before she went through with it in April of 1993. Each time he convinced her to hang around longer than she expected. Even when divorced, she kept in touch with him. Her strong-willed, stubborn attitude disappeared when she was around Andrew and from what I could tell he satisfied her every need, including drugs. I believe she did the same for him. Their drug of choice was crystal methamphetamine but I am sure that whatever was available would do. Andrew's claim of being a recovering alcoholic and drug user was unbelievable. His actions were not those of a sober person. His mannerisms were like my sister's when she was high. I knew he was on something most of the time and I believe that is why my intuition told me to stay away.

After her divorce, Stephanie took up with another man named Raymond Gomez. Raymond had known mom and my step-dad for many years before Stephanie moved in with him. He had three children, ranging in age from ten to seventeen. Stephanie and his oldest were close in age.

July 9, 1993

Stephanie and Raymond, along with his two younger children, drove to the lake with some friends to spend a few days in the Arizona sun swimming, boating and camping. It saddens me to realize that instead of being fun, the trip turned violent. Raymond became aggressive towards Stephanie. A combination of drinking, possibly drugs, and the need to show-off made this a most unpleasant getaway. A couple of months earlier, Stephanie had seen the doctor about pain in her right knee. She told the doctor that her injury was from playing Frisbee but we later learned that Raymond was responsible. He had a history of violent behavior before he met Stephanie.

July 11, 1993

Another violent incident occurred during that trip. To escape further harm, she waited until he left on the boat to go fishing. Then she took his vehicle and left him and his children there. Since they were with a large group, Raymond and the kids would have a way home. Later that evening, when Stephanie was back at mom's house, they heard Raymond in the front yard. He was in a rage, trashing her truck, punching, kicking, and throwing things. He was insistent that she come outside. She was afraid but knew she had to face him. She asked mom to go with her. He was intimidating, flexing his muscles and sweating profusely from his anger. As he lunged towards her, mom ordered him to leave the property. My step-dad backed her up and Raymond finally left. Stephanie filed charges.

3 | THE BEGINNING OF THE END

July 12, 1993

Raymond called Stephanie and apologized for his behavior and for injuring her knee. She accepted his apology, and dropped the charges. They agreed to end their relationship since it wasn't healthy. He offered to pay the bill for the doctor's visit but she refused. To take her mind off the breakup, she decided to take a trip with Andrew and told Raymond. It was a couple of weeks in Southern California and the Pacific Northwest up toward Canada.

July 13, 1993

Andrew and Stephanie left and stopped by my dad's place in Southern California. I am glad dad was able to see her one last time.

July 28, 1993

When she returned from their vacation, she was home less than an hour before she was arrested for theft and forgery. Earlier in the month, Raymond filed a complaint at the police station, stating, "Stephanie took several checks from my house that I signed and she cashed them for her own use. I did not give her my permission." Apparently when Stephanie left the lake, she drove to his house and took the checks. Raymond said, "I signed the checks for my son, Raymond Gomez, Jr., to use in case of an emergency. My son told me that he saw Stephanie at the house." Raymond was notified by a bank teller that Stephanie cashed a check for $1,500.00. The memo section of the check read, "fishing trip." The five checks she wrote amounted to $2,400.00. Two were made out to cash and three were to her, in her own handwriting.

To be spiteful, she sent him several postcards from her trip, one stating, 'Makin' lots of $.' She mocked him for financing their vacation. At the police department, he expressed remorse for his treatment of her.

Stephanie spent only one night in jail and her court date was scheduled for August 23, 1993. She was released on her own recognizance and was to stay with mom. Stephanie couldn't maintain her lifestyle at mom and our step-dad's house. She asked mom if she could instead stay with Andrew until her court date. Her manipulation worked because mom agreed. Stephanie would call mom every evening to check in. We both talked to mom everyday anyway. Mom now regrets letting her go, and feels responsible for what happened. When Stephanie left to stay with Andrew, she promised to call every day and she did until August 18th.

August 16, 1993

The last time I spoke to Stephanie was when I went by Andrew's house to pick up a video camera for a baby shower I was attending. She was nice enough to allow me to borrow it. The last time mom talked to her was August 17.

August 18, 1993

Andrew contacted mom at 12:30 p.m. and mom wondered why it took him nine hours to tell her Stephanie was missing. He claimed that he had been trying to call her office all morning but only reached the answering machine.

Mom later learned that granny had called Andrew looking for Stephanie around 11:30 a.m. and that was when he asked for mom's work number. We couldn't understand why he told mom he had been calling her office all morning when he told granny he didn't have mom's work number. If it was that dire, he could have told granny that Stephanie had been missing since that morning, but he didn't. Or he could have gone to mom's office.

The confusion and panic were mounting by the minute. I found it hard to breathe and my heart was pounding. I do not remember ever feeling such intense fear. It got worse when I realized the terror mom was feeling. We didn't know what to do or where to turn. I followed mom's lead, trusting that she would find her daughter safe and sound.

It was now that evening and because Andrew had injured Stephanie in the past, more red flags went up. Andrew's strange behavior was confusing. Mom decided to go out to Heckle Road and search for Stephanie. Because Andrew had lied, mom began to fear the worst. He wasn't making sense and was insistent that mom report her missing to the Sheriff's Office.

August 19, 1993 (Missing for 1 day)

In the morning hours, mom and granny again went to Heckle Road to look for Stephanie. They found no sign of her. They then drove to granny's house and mom called my sister's attorney, Mariah Stannage. She offered to contact a few people who might have information on her disappearance. Mom called Andrew to tell him that Mariah had been informed. Granny called Raymond to ask if he had heard from her. Mom knew Raymond but because he filed charges against my sister she refused to communicate with him.

Andrew showed up at granny's house uninvited. More red flags went up when his story sounded odd and he didn't recall details. For some reason, he wanted to talk about the new boots he had purchased. The conversation then turned to the drugs she was using. We tried to learn what type of drugs they were, but he wouldn't say. He insisted we make no mention of her drug use to the Sheriff's Office. This convinced mom he was lying.

Since being released from jail, Stephanie had only been in the presence of Andrew and mom. Mom wouldn't have given her drugs and we believed Andrew when he said that he no longer used alcohol and drugs.

When Mariah called back, she told mom to file a missing person's report. The prosecutor would not view her as a runaway because Andrew had admitted to being the last person to see her alive. Andrew was asked to join mom at the Sheriff's Department to give his statement. He agreed to meet them there later.

When mom and granny arrived, Andrew was already giving his statement to a Deputy. He repeated that she had left the vehicle upset, and he left her there, the last person to see her alive. His statement sounded rehearsed. Mom became more suspicious when he couldn't remember what she was wearing, except the black high tops.

Mom refused to look at him and granny had to walk away to compose herself. The Deputy said he would have the location searched later in the day. After hearing Andrew state he left a Gatorade bottle with Stephanie, mom told the Deputy she'd noticed it out there but hadn't realized its

3 | THE BEGINNING OF THE END

importance.

Since Andrew's behavior was suspicious and his statement implied foul play, and the Deputy wasn't going to go out to the area until later in the day, mom and granny drove back to Heckle Road to locate the Gatorade bottle. They found the bottle and took it in to the Sheriff's Office, handling it carefully to preserve any potential fingerprints.

Andrew insisted that both he and Stephanie had been drinking the Gatorade on the way to the hot tubs but mom and granny noticed that the seal hadn't been broken. Mom was later notified that because of the bottle type, fingerprints could not be recovered.

We were alarmed when we learned that Andrew was selling Stephanie's truck. It was on his property and he claimed that he had done work on it. He either wasn't a good mechanic or was lying because it was an older vehicle and didn't run. The lack of honesty was disturbing. Andrew wasn't authorized to sell her property, and his decision to get rid of it had a darker implication. We asked ourselves, "How does he know that Stephanie isn't going to show up and claim the truck?"

I was not involved in the search efforts and investigation. My twins were two years old and my daughter was seven. We were kept out of the public eye so my family could be safe and my new job as a Federal Law Enforcement Officer wouldn't be compromised. It was a relief to be free from the drama. My full-time job, taking care of my young children and my household responsibilities kept me from worrying about Stephanie. Staying busy was my way of maintaining sanity in the chaos.

I wondered what could have happened to her. Keeping my thoughts to myself wasn't therapeutic, but I had to focus on my life and not the fear. I was afraid for Stephanie and tried to stay positive for mom. We didn't know if Stephanie was alive or dead but I tried to remember the good times we had together.

One memory that always brought a smile was when we had a photograph taken of us just two months before her disappearance. It was her idea and because of our history, I didn't want to do it. But I went ahead because it was to be a surprise present for mom's July birthday. We had a great time during the photo session, laughing and joking, so for that I am grateful. That was the last picture taken of us together. It's almost as if she knew she was going to die. Suggesting we pose together for a professional photograph was unusual for Stephanie. Little did I know it was going to be the last image of her. I have it displayed in my curio cabinet surrounded by angel figurines.

CHAPTER FOUR
The Craziness Starts

Mom returned home the afternoon of the 19th to a ringing telephone. That screeching noise became a sound mom loathed. When the phone would ring, the muscles in her neck and shoulders would tense up, and the pain became constant. I could hear the tension in her voice. She would answer, not knowing if it was more rumor and speculation, if Stephanie was calling, or if law enforcement had new information. This time it was Andrew on the other end of the line.

"Were you out on Heckle Road and if so, did you take the Gatorade bottle that was out there?"

Mom said, "Yes, we were on Heckle Road and I took it to the Sheriff's Office."

"What shoes were you and your mom wearing?" Mom described their footwear.

Andrew stated, "I am out here with a Deputy looking around." At that point, the conversation ended.

It was confusing as we didn't understand why Andrew was asking those questions and not the Deputies. It was strange that the person who admitted to being the last to see her alive was now leading the investigation.

Mom couldn't believe that a Deputy would allow

Andrew to question her for information on a potential crime scene. She decided to verify the Deputy's presence and contacted the dispatcher. They said that a Deputy was sent to Heckle Road.

When she hung up, mom's fear intensified. She asked granny and me to go with her to the area. Mom called Andrew to tell him we were going to meet them. He seemed determined to keep us from coming. He told mom the Deputy was leaving for the evening.

After they hung up, mom was conflicted. She decided to act on her intuition and go anyway. When we arrived, the Deputy was still there and the only one who had left was Andrew. The Deputy said a tracking team had followed footprints to the cattle guard, about .7 miles from the main highway. The trackers assumed that these were Stephanie's prints and that she had been picked up. The Deputy stated that he would put out an ATL (attempt to locate) for her and request an air search the next day.

The Deputy asked mom if she knew whether Stephanie had spent a week in Duncan with friends within the last couple of months. Duncan is about 40 miles east of our town, with a population of 700 people, three miles from the New Mexico border. Mom couldn't recall Stephanie having friends there.

Mom believed that if Stephanie were able, she would have called by now. I also believed that to be true. Stephanie would want to know if her birthday money had arrived from our grandmother on our dad's side.

I asked the Deputy if he had brought the dogs out during the search to verify that Stephanie had been there. He said that he hadn't.

They had tracked prints from the vehicle. It appeared that Stephanie had hidden behind nearby brush. The prints seemed to go back to the road and the main highway. I didn't understand how they could be so sure that these were Stephanie's. In light of Andrew's background, his word couldn't be trusted. And without hard evidence, we couldn't assume anything.

After leaving the area, mom, granny and I went home hoping Stephanie had tried to contact us. Unfortunately, no messages were left.

Later that evening, Andrew paid granny a visit. He told granny that Stephanie had a female lover in Duncan and that she had spent a week with this woman. According to Andrew, Stephanie wanted her to stay at Andrew's to have a three-way sexual encounter. Andrew agreed to go along with it only because he wanted to please Stephanie. I do not understand why he would tell granny this story. Even if true, that's not what a grandmother wants to hear about her grandchild. He must have had an underlying motive since it had no bearing on the investigation. If she was in Duncan, she would have called mom. We thought he was manipulating granny for more information.

The Sheriff's Office should have asked granny about this woman, not Andrew. They did locate the girl to determine if she had seen Stephanie recently. Unfortunately, she had not. Andrew went back to granny's house but granny refused to answer the door.

August 20, 1993 (Missing for 2 days)

Mom contacted the Deputy to ask if there were any new developments. He said an air search was considered but with no evidence of foul play at the scene, it was scrapped. Raymond was nice enough to fund an air search. They found no sign of Stephanie. Raymond's relationship with her had been strained, but he loved her and wanted her found. This was his way of doing what he could.

Mom asked the Deputy what the priority of the case was now, and he said low. Because they thought she made it to the highway, she was considered a runaway.

Mom contacted dad to see if he had heard from her and he had not. The last time he saw her was when she and Andrew stopped by in mid-July.

August 21, 1993 (Missing for 3 days)

The following Saturday, mom contacted the Sheriff's Deputy and asked if the prints could indicate an injury on the right foot. Stephanie had broken her foot and on June 9, she had surgery to re-break the foot so it would heal properly. She had been wearing a soft cast because it hadn't healed completely. The Deputy stated that the tracks they believed were Stephanie's were so faint that they only detected a print every 10 to 15 steps.

August 22, 1993 (Missing for 4 days)

Mom continued to review Andrew's story and thought it had too many holes to be believable. Mom and I went out to Heckle Road again and spent an hour searching but found nothing. It was eerie to think we were standing where she might have spent her last moments on earth.

Later that day mom called Andrew and asked him to explain why he thought she was using drugs. He said she had mood swings, but Stephanie had always been moody. We knew to give her space.

He asked mom if she had a pair of Stephanie's jeans to complete an outfit in case she showed up for her court hearing the next day.

He said he was excited about her possible return and wanted to purchase a card to welcome her home.

He asked mom for dad's phone number. Later when I spoke with dad, he thought Andrew's call was strange, because he hadn't sounded genuinely concerned. Andrew spoke as if he were reading from a book. The conversation was awkward at best since they had only met once. I talked to dad regularly to keep him informed of new developments. Maybe Andrew was trying to learn what we knew from dad.

This is where the spiritual aspect of our story begins. That night about 9:30 p.m., I had a strange feeling that someone was watching me. My then husband, Roger, was a few blocks away at his cousin's house. I was home alone with my young children, who were asleep, and my heart began racing. All I wanted to do was climb into bed with my children and pull the covers over my head, but since they were sleeping soundly in their beds, I called Roger. I pleaded for him to come home, saying I was afraid. I knew Stephanie was with me.

I wasn't sure spirits contacted the living so my fear overpowered my gratitude. I was grateful that she had come, but I was too frightened to receive any message. Instead, I begged Roger to drive home and he finally did, about an hour after I called.

I told Roger about my experience that night and he

laughed it off, saying I was imagining things. The next day I told mom about the encounter and she said I was just upset and processing stress. Adding to that, my twins were ill.

All my responsibilities and worries just got the best of me. But I knew it was her. I couldn't explain it, since I didn't know how this could be possible. I couldn't check the internet for similar experiences because it wasn't invented yet.

I discounted my intuition and believed my family, and when later events proved me right, I learned the value of my gut instinct. That sixth sense protects and informs us.

CHAPTER FIVE
Stephanie Makes Her Presence Known

The day of Stephanie's court hearing, I was desperate to learn what had happened to her. I was hoping to get the answers in court. I couldn't help but feel sad for mom as she was smoking again while she waited for my sister's attorney. She was staring off into space and I wondered what she would say if Stephanie were to walk up. Mom was prepared for the worst, but hoping for the best, and that would be Stephanie's return. This ordeal was heart-wrenching. My mother had lost her child, and we didn't know if Stephanie was alive or dead. We wanted her back or at the very least, her body to be found.

Mom wanted to speak to Mariah about Andrew's involvement with Stephanie's disappearance and possible death. His physical abuse of Stephanie in the past made his inconsistent and strange behavior seem incriminating.

Stephanie had an appendectomy in October 1989, and about a month later, he had taken her to Phoenix and held her there against her will for three days. During that time, he beat her with a crowbar. Mom spoke to us both regularly and when she hadn't heard from Stephanie, she began to worry. Andrew was arrested for a probation violation because he assaulted my sister. He was also charged with failure to participate in his Alcoholic Anonymous meeting, consumption of intoxicating liquors, and possession and use of illegal drugs.

Stephanie had now been gone for five days and we'd already found 21 discrepancies in his story. Because of the length of her disappearance, the history of Andrew's behavior toward her, and the inconsistencies in his story, Mariah advised mom that after the hearing to find an article of Stephanie's clothing, take it to the Sheriff's Office and request that the investigator bring dogs out to Heckle Road. It was then that mom realized Andrew was the main suspect.

Stephanie's hearing began without her being present. Because she did not show up, the court asked mom if she objected to a bench warrant being issued with a bond of $1,000.00 set for Stephanie's arrest. Mom approved the order, but Andrew objected, and I wondered if it was because her name and information would be added to the criminal database. Since Stephanie was divorced from him, he didn't have a legal right to prevent the warrant from being issued.

Andrew did not know that we would be meeting an investigator with the Sheriff's Office after the court hearing. The officer said that he would ask if the dogs were available and get back with us.

In the meantime, mom, granny and I returned to Heckle Road. When we arrived, we couldn't believe that she had been out there, it just didn't make sense. The story Andrew told us wasn't logical. We stayed out on that dirt road trying to imagine what could have happened. We wondered if she had stood where we were now, or if she hadn't been out there at all. Only one person could answer that question, the last to see her alive, but it was obvious he would divulge nothing more. We drove back to granny's house where we waited for the investigator to notify us if the dogs would be sent out to the scene.

Granny contacted my uncle. My uncle was mom's younger brother who lived in the Phoenix area but has now passed. From the age of three or four, he received premonitions through dreams. Granny experienced this as well. Other members of my family on mom's side have psychic gifts. Some are able to contact spirits who have crossed over and some are like granny and my uncle who dream about close friends and family. Mom asked if he'd had any strange dreams recently.

Nobody had told him Stephanie was missing yet, but he replied, "Norma, it is funny you should ask me that. On Tuesday or Wednesday of last week, I had a dream that dad came to visit me and we went for a ride in his new two-toned blue van. When he took me home, a girl named Stacey was there and I told her how happy I was to see her and that her mother was worried about her." (My uncle was dating a woman whose daughter was murdered in the Phoenix area. The girl's name was Stacey).

Mom told him about Stephanie and he said the girl in his dream could have been Stephanie. That made more sense because Stacey had died several years earlier. Later, I saw a picture of Stacey and the two girls bore an uncanny resemblance. Since I do not believe in coincidences, I am convinced Stephanie was connecting with my uncle through this dream.

My uncle suggested we call a psychic medium who

helped his girlfriend find her missing daughter. Her name was Gina St. Claire. Gina was from the mid-west and had been a professional psychic medium for 12 years. She had been featured on television documentaries locating missing loved ones and worked with law enforcement in solving unexplained murders.

Mom liked the idea and contacted her on August 25th. When she introduced herself to Gina, mom told her about Stephanie.

Gina asked, "Are the police involved with this case?" Gina said she felt an absence of law enforcement.

"Yes," mom answered.

"What is your daughter's full name?" Gina wanted more energy, she explained.

"Originally it was Stephanie Ann Johnson, but her last name was changed to Stephanie Ann Proffitt in 1979."

"What is the color of her hair?" Gina asked.

"Brown," mom answered.

"I believe that there are two men in Stephanie's life. One has messy dark hair and the other has long blond hair and he works quite a bit."

"Yes."

"I believe that the blond one has a business involving cars. I do not feel that either one is connected to her death. I am not sure how the blond passed the polygraph. I do not believe that Stephanie was ever out on Heckle Road."

Mom replied, "That is how I felt. Can you tell us if she is dead? I believe she is gone. I have a hole in my heart that tells me that she is no longer in the physical world."

"She is now at peace," Gina replied. "Have the Sheriff

5 | STEPHANIE MAKES HER PRESENCE KNOWN

contact the Tempe police and they will verify my role in the case of Stacey."

Gina added, "Send me something of Stephanie's that was special to her and send pictures of Stephanie, Andrew, and Raymond."

"I will send a necklace, a blanket and her shoes, along with pictures," Mom told her. "I'm glad you'll help in the investigation."

The worst that could happen would be that she failed to contribute new information. At this point, we were willing to try anything.

August 28, 1993 (Missing 10 days)

Mom received a phone call from the Sheriff stating that he had spoken with Gina. She felt Stephanie made it back to the highway and was picked up by a Hispanic male Stephanie knew, but not well. He wanted to have sex with her but she refused so the man raped and killed her. Gina felt that her body was in a stock pond near an abandoned adobe house. An area fitting that description was located within three to six miles of where she was last seen. Several people went with mom to that area where they searched for 12 hours, with no results. As you can imagine, mom was devastated.

Gina wouldn't work with mom after that. She did not feel comfortable with the Sheriff. She didn't give further details to us or the Sheriff's Office.

I believe that because I was too afraid to help her, Stephanie reached out to my uncle. Although it did not affect the case, we were grateful that my uncle connected with her.

I had another encounter. I was dozing on mom's couch and suddenly felt like I was on the Disneyland ride, Space Mountain. I was speeding through a tunnel, and as it started to slow, a picture began to materialize. The first vision was a barrel cactus with a beautiful, bright orange bloom. The second was a long slender black box, large enough to hold a person, similar to a coffin. This was made of cheap wood and spray-painted black, with one end shaped in a half-diamond. The last image was of a man with a sleeveless denim shirt but I could only see his chest, not his face. I still do not know if this was relevant. It seemed so real at the time that I trusted the vision.

I also trusted that Stephanie did not want us to know the details, as they would not bring her back. She just wanted us to forgive her and be at peace with what had happened. Easier said than done.

August 30, 1993 (Missing 12 days)

Mom's friends and coworkers began making and distributing flyers to post in our county and the two adjacent counties, but the result was only a few leads. Our family appreciated the efforts of all those who took the time to help our family.

I had another psychic contact that night around 9:00 p.m. I was in bed trying to fall asleep when I had the sensation of a weight pressing down on the bed. It felt as though someone was sitting at my feet and I noticed the light depression of the mattress. My eyes were closed so I thought it might be my husband. Even though I was covered by the blankets with my head on the pillow, I knew there was a presence with me.

I had the feeling of someone watching me and I was guided to talk to Stephanie. I wasn't sure what to say as this was new to me. I tried to rationalize this as a simple exchange of words, except I would talk and the responses would pop into my head. I was aware of sensations on my body that convinced me she was real.

I asked her to give me a sign, and a belt hanging in the corner began to sway and a plant also began to move. Chills traveled up and down my body and at that moment, because I did not understand the process of connecting with a passed loved one, I again became fearful.

With my thoughts, I asked her to help us. I was told to forgive her, and that she was okay. I had the impression that she didn't want us to know what happened as she felt ashamed. I tried to close my eyes and sleep but continued to experience this connection. The next impression was stronger, and I knew that she did not want us to worry and again, didn't want us to know the details. In reality, the circumstances didn't matter, I knew that she was gone.

September 1, 1993 (Missing 14 days)

Since I was running late for work, I decided to wash my hair in the tub. I was sitting on my knees, with my head under the faucet. I felt a sting on my lower back and tried to brush it off. It started to throb and burn, and I wondered if a scorpion had stung me. As I finished drying my hair, I looked in the mirror but couldn't see that area, so I asked my seven-year-old daughter what it was. It was still burning, stinging and tingling. She said, "Mom, it looks like you were slapped on your back because it has three finger marks." She held up her hand and showed me three fingers, the index, middle, and ring fingers. The sensation lasted all day.

I didn't know how to process this, but I knew it was Stephanie, especially since I had recently communicated with her. Again, I didn't know much about the connection between the physical and spiritual worlds, and was still afraid.

That day, mom and granny were discussing Stephanie, now a missing person, at least according to the Sheriff's report, while others speculated she could be a runaway. Some felt that she was evading a possible prison sentence. Because we had no answers from the Sheriff's Office, mom called the Department of Public Safety to enlist their help. They said the Sheriff's Office had to ask for their assistance with the investigation. Mom also wrote a letter to the State of Arizona Attorney General's Office. Like the Department of Public Safety, they were unable to provide any resources unless requested by the Sheriff.

Later that evening about 8:45 p.m., my daughter and my twin boys were asleep in the living room. My daughter and one of the twins lay on the floor while the other twin was curled up against my chest on the couch. I was watching television and heard a moan and the sound of scratching. The twin sleeping with me woke up and looked around. I then heard a sound in the master bathroom, getting louder. At that point, I became terrified and turned up the volume on the television. The noises eventually went away.

I felt conflicted because I didn't know what she wanted but I was also fearful. This had to be her, I had never heard noises in that house before then. I was frustrated because I didn't know how to help her and at the same time I wondered if this was all a product of my imagination. She must have been frustrated as well since she was trying to communicate but I couldn't understand her.

The next day we received a copy of a memorandum that listed what the investigator and a Deputy from the Sheriff's Office had done thus far to find my sister. I was disappointed when I read that they'd only taken 12 actions. Stephanie had been missing for 15 days.

Work and my family responsibilities kept my emotions in check. I didn't want to scare my kids, cry and act like a crazy person. I didn't want to fall apart when she was really alive and this was just another dirty trick. But I had a sense that she had left the physical world and her soul was at peace. Because this was all new to me, I didn't trust my intuition. She now had no pain or sorrow and I envied that. I stayed busy caring for my kids and going to work, ignoring the worry and grief.

Mom was angry and decided to solve this case on her own. She wasn't angry at the entire Sheriff's Department, just a few key players. She thought they weren't taking Stephanie's disappearance seriously due to her reputation. My family knew that Stephanie didn't run away, we were convinced that Andrew killed her and then disposed of her body. We decided to not have further contact with Andrew.

In the middle of the night, granny received a phone call. The caller disguised his voice and granny was ordered to stop telling lies or she would be killed. Granny was so scared she bought a gun the next day. This all seemed like a movie or television show, but it was our reality.

Mom and I were interviewed by a Phoenix television station and the Arizona Republic. We hoped public awareness would put pressure on the Sheriff to ask other government departments for assistance.

There was more information coming in. Mom received calls saying that Andrew had been seen shooting Stephanie up with drugs. Some of the stories were investigated by the Sheriff's Office and some weren't.

CHAPTER SIX
Going Nowhere

The Sheriff would activate Stephanie's investigation only when false leads came in and September 7 was no different. The Sheriff notified mom of security footage showing a girl stealing cigarettes at the convenience store. Andrew and Stephanie had been in the vicinity the night they were on Heckle Road, and the Sheriff thought this might be Stephanie.

Mom rushed to town muttering, *please,* under her breath, but when she viewed the tape it was obviously not Stephanie. She wanted to see the videotape of the night Stephanie disappeared. We were surprised to learn the Sheriff's Department hadn't considered this. It was baffling that they wanted her to see a girl that might be Stephanie stealing cigarettes, but not the video of the night she disappeared. The sheriff should have followed that lead immediately after hearing Andrew's account.

When she did view the tape from when Stephanie was reported missing, mom saw a man with physical characteristics similar to Andrew's enter the store at about 2:55 a.m. He was wearing black hightops similar to Stephanie's. She informed the Sheriff and on September 8, the man was identified as Andrew. There was a two-hour time discrepancy noted in his story. It now made sense to me why the Sheriff hadn't told mom about this. I would like to know if the Sheriff had already viewed it and was aware of this inconsistency, but didn't want it disclosed.

Mom decided to work with a Deputy she trusted more than the Sheriff. The Sheriff was condescending when we'd ask questions and beg him to include other law enforcement agencies. By doing so they could utilize more resources. Based on Andrew's story, Stephanie was last seen alive on federal land. The FBI should have been involved, but for some reason the Sheriff refused to notify them.

Mom continued to write letters to the Governor's Office, the Graham County Attorney's Office, the State of Arizona Attorney General's Office and the United States Attorney General's Office, a Senator from our district, the Graham County Board of Supervisors, and the Department of Public Safety. The list goes on, but they all had the same response. They could not help without the Sheriff's request. This was proof to us that he had something to hide.

Mom and I went to the Sheriff's Office on September 9 to ask for a copy of the NCIC (National Crime Information Center) report, but were denied access. We were informed that the initial police report stated her name would be entered because she was a missing person.

I received another one of my feelings the morning of September 15. I was in the shower getting ready for work and I had the feeling that Stephanie was frustrated with us. She was giving us signs but we weren't receiving them. I again felt someone watching me, my left arm began to tingle and I felt chills in my body. As quickly as these feelings appeared, they disappeared. I went on about my day and forgot about the strange episode, although I recorded it in my journal.

We reviewed the memorandum submitted on September 15 by one of the Deputies. We could not comprehend why it had taken one hour to enter her original information in the NCIC database. We were told that it was updated to include a bench warrant and that it was issued when she failed to appear in court. But we still had not received a copy despite having requested it.

When I approached one of my mentors at work for advice on the case, he said we should demand a copy of the NCIC from the Sheriff. We had believed the Sheriff when he stated that we weren't allowed to have a copy. My mentor advised me differently.

He asked someone from Human Resources to run my sister's name in the database. The employee refused, saying he would only access the NCIC on official business. When my mentor gave him a direct order to issue a report, he complied.

Upon receiving it, I could see the information was incorrect. This explained why the Sheriff would not let us have a copy. At that point, my mentor suggested we make an appointment with the Sheriff for the report. We were to act as though we had not seen it and not disclose what we knew.

I met mom later that day and she also looked at the NCIC report, agreeing that none of the information on Stephanie was accurate. The weight listed on the NCIC was 20 pounds heavier. There were no identifying marks noted on the NCIC although she had three tattoos, one on each leg and one on her stomach. The NCIC report stated there were no outstanding warrants and there was nothing indicating that she was a missing person.

When we arrived at the Sheriff's Office, mom demanded that the Sheriff run the NCIC for us. We were curious to see how he would respond. We waited for what seemed like hours before he returned with a copy. He claimed he had to update the information for accuracy. This was more proof that he was either involved in her disappearance and death, or he was protecting Andrew. Maybe both.

The discrepancies and lies gave us reason to believe that the Sheriff and Andrew were working together and my sister had been somehow involved in their scheme. I guess the Sheriff didn't expect mom, granny and me to be so proactive.

The days continued with no contact from Stephanie nor did we receive any news from the Sheriff's Office. It had almost been a month and the hope that she would be found alive was fading.

It takes someone with a big ego to believe that they are above the law with no concern for human life. It seemed as though Andrew and the Sheriff didn't care that she was missing.

We thought it puzzling that the Sheriff allowed Andrew, who left her out in the desert and was "the last to see her alive," access to the investigation. I would think that he would do all he could to find a girl who had been declared missing in his county. Other resources were available but he chose not to make use of them. Andrew was becoming more defensive and paranoid.

Other rumors surfaced about my sister and as I read the details in mom's journal my heart sank. The tips on my sister's disappearance were all phoned in to mom. On three occasions mom heard that Stephanie's body had been found and each report proved to be false. The roller coaster of emotion continued.

A few days later, Andrew lost his temper and became furious with mom. He learned that mom and granny were making burial arrangements for my sister. But he had no say in the matter.

Mom was convinced Stephanie was gone. Stephanie would have contacted us by now if she were alive. She would have wanted her birthday money from grandma or drugs from Andrew or Raymond. When Stephanie's body was recovered, mom would be overcome with emotion, so she wanted to plan the funeral beforehand.

At the cemetery mom and granny choose a plot where most of the family on mom's side is buried. Granny's dad whom I always called Grandpa Mailman was buried there along with some of granny's sisters. Granny had reserved a plot there for herself. A space for Stephanie was designated right above granny's. I know this was difficult for mom. Children are supposed to bury their parents, not the other way around.

Dad wasn't involved and that was probably a good thing. With their emotions running high, who knows what might have happened between mom and dad. He has guilt for contributing to her lifestyle, but he runs from stress. He has been criticized for his actions as a parent. People deal with stress in their own way and his choices were different from mom's.

Some people may judge mom and I am sure she has judged others. I heard people say, "How dare she plan a funeral, Stephanie might come home alive."

Mom did her best to protect me and my family by making the decisions she did. Stephanie was murdered and even though we believe it was her ex-husband who killed her, we do not know. Whoever it was, they were still out there and mom didn't want them to come after me and my family. The grim reality at that point was Stephanie was probably dead, although we still hoped she was alive.

Mom planned a beautiful service, but Andrew said Stephanie wanted to be cremated. Since Stephanie had divorced him he could not make that decision. We suspected Andrew wanted her cremated because he didn't want her body autopsied. It was telling that he was so determined and it validated our belief that he was involved in her disappearance. Since it didn't matter what he wanted, mom proceeded with her arrangements.

According to mom's journals, she contacted a former legislator on September 14, who told her that the Sheriff's Office should have requested outside help long before now. He advised her to call the Governor's Office. She was told by that office that she should contact the Chairman of the Board of Supervisors. Granny called the Chairman and was told that the Sheriff had no superiors, he answered to the people. Mom and granny asked the community to write to the newspaper and the Sheriff's Office.

The Justice of the Peace found an A.R.S. code that would give mom possession of Stephanie's property. Mariah completed the necessary paperwork for the court.

Stephanie had now been missing for 27 days and none

of her belongings had been returned to my family. Mom called the Director of the Department of Public Safety but was told they did not participate in investigations. They suggested that mom call the County Attorney's Office. The County Attorney said he had no authority over the Sheriff but he said to call the Department of Public Safety.

Mom explained, "I realize that Stephanie didn't lead a perfect life, but she was my daughter and 27 days is too long to not know if she was murdered."

He said, "I have not heard derogatory remarks made about your daughter. I will contact the Sheriff to ask that he enlist the aid of the Department of Public Safety."

During one of our meetings with the Sheriff, I said, "I am very aware of how Stephanie lived her life. I know she wasn't the best person, but we need to know her whereabouts."

Tears filled my eyes and my voice wavered, but I continued, "She deserves to be found, and the person responsible for doing her harm should be punished."

This would be another indication that the Sheriff was involved in her death. He answered, "Yes, if not for your sister, then for you and your mother."

There was still no news, good or bad, but mom needed closure. She feared that her daughter's body would never be found.

Mom spoke to the Undersheriff and learned that he might bring in an impartial person or team from the Department of Public Safety not familiar with this area, since the Sheriff had run out of leads.

Mom asked if someone would enlarge the film from the convenience store so she could get a better view of the hightops Andrew wore. She believed those shoes belonged to Stephanie. He originally said that he was wearing the bluish-gray boots that night. Based on the film, he was wearing tennis shoes. We gave this evidence to the Sheriff, but like the other leads, it wasn't investigated. This gave us more reason to believe the Sheriff didn't want Stephanie found.

September 16, 1993 (Missing 29 days)

In the early evening mom called the Undersheriff for new developments, but there was none. He reminded mom that he needed a body before there was an actual crime and she pleaded for him not to give up. He seemed to imply he was the only one interested in this case. Mom was desperate, frustrated, and wanted this nightmare to end.

Mom remembered another person in the area who was psychic. This person knew Andrew and was afraid he would kill her if he learned that she was talking to mom about Stephanie. Mom visited her and the woman said she knew Stephanie and had always felt sorry for her because Andrew beat her. She had received visions of Stephanie's murder and was waiting for mom to contact her. She believed Andrew murdered Stephanie and that her body was in an area west of town. She said she once witnessed Andrew beating Stephanie and knew he was capable of killing her in a rage. She felt that Raymond had nothing to do with her disappearance.

The psychic promised to call mom back in a couple of days. Mom hoped that she would have an exact location for Stephanie as she put more trust in the medium's abilities than the Sheriff's Office.

More information was coming from people in our community. It was all conjecture, but mom wanted every lead followed. Someone mom worked with said her husband was at a local store in the hardware department and overheard Andrew talking down the aisle from him. Andrew said that you could hit her again and again and she would keep coming back, but she had met her maker with a .357 Magnum. Mom called the Sheriff's Deputy she trusted and repeated the statement. He said they knew Andrew owned a .9MM, and so that lead wasn't pursued.

We realized they couldn't follow all the wild claims, but everything about this case was out of the ordinary. Andrew said he was the last person to see her alive and had left her in the desert, knowing that she wasn't in her right mind. Now, he was an active participant in the investigation. This was not only illogical but inconceivable.

That afternoon, another relative called to say Andrew was asking about a backhoe that could dig a hole 14-feet deep. He had met with a local businessman who sold double-wides and owned a trailer park. Mom repeated this to the Undersheriff who promised to have someone keep an eye on Andrew over the weekend.

The Undersheriff was going to be busy with a protest on our mountain the Department of Public Safety would also cover. Mom prayed that they would focus attention on Stephanie's disappearance, since the protest fell under the jurisdiction of other law enforcement agencies. Every day that went by increased the likelihood that her body would never be found.

That evening, a friend of granny's came to see her who was familiar with Stephanie's case. Earlier in the month, a rumor started that Stephanie had been found in a well and she had been stabbed or shot in the back. Four people called to tell mom this. Each of them said that an Emergency Medical Technician (EMT) in town had found her but no one knew his name.

A week or so later mom called the ambulance company and repeated what she'd heard. One of their ambulance workers told people there he helped take Stephanie out of the well, despite the Sheriff's Office insistence that this wasn't true. This man was an EMT and also worked for a doctor, and he said the body had been found and that the police wanted to keep it from the public.

The Sheriff's Office was going to conduct a drug raid before they released the news that they had found her. This led us back to our belief that Andrew was their informant, and we wondered if the Sheriff's office was withholding information on Stephanie until this huge drug bust took place. If Stephanie was found before the raid was carried out, then Andrew would not be willing to cooperate with the Sheriff. Stephanie had to be found after the sting operation.

This man also told granny that the police were watching Raymond, Andrew, and another person who had known Stephanie. They were under surveillance 24 hours a day, and the sheriffs suspected one of them was responsible for her disappearance. From what this man disclosed, we thought the police knew one of them stabbed or shot her in the back.

This added to the frustration we had with the Sheriff's Office. Mom and granny were bombarded by phone calls and people stating they knew what happened to Stephanie.

September 18, 1993 (Missing 31 days)

The Sheriff made an announcement on the local radio news that Stephanie was still missing and anyone with information on her disappearance should contact his department. He said someone might call in with that one piece of evidence that would lead to Stephanie's being found.

Everyone mom talked to believed that Andrew had killed her. Andrew's ex-girlfriend, who had a child with him, gave a statement to the Undersheriff that Andrew had tried to kill her a number of times. She also informed mom of this.

Mom met with another local psychic. I believe they have a heightened sense of intuition because I do. Mom was desperate for answers and although some mediums offer accurate information, mom's need for the truth made her vulnerable. Most of those who gave us tips were well-intentioned, but some were not. This can only be discerned by intuition.

Determining which leads should be reported to the authorities, which should be kept from the Sheriff's office, and which should be dismissed altogether was exhausting.

This psychic said that he put his mind into Stephanie's body. He felt someone throwing dirt on him. He said he was in a trench as deep as a man is tall. He then moved to the other end of the trench and a glass wall surrounded him and the weight of the dirt was lighter.

People forgot that this was her flesh and blood and they used graphic images. If the community had trusted the Sheriff's Office maybe they wouldn't have given the gruesome reports to mom.

Mom met with someone else offering information. "Your phone is being tapped on your incoming calls," she explained. "I believe that it is the police checking to see if Stephanie called." She was right in a way. Mom did have a recorder to pick up incoming calls.

"Andrew is being watched 24 hours a day but it may not be by an actual Deputy, but rather someone the Sheriff's Office has hired to watch him."

She continued, "If his house were to be searched, all of his videotapes should be seized, as I see that Andrew may be exploiting Stephanie in exchange for drugs."

If this was true, how disgusting that my sister would be involved with a man who would do that.

This caller continued, "Stephanie is dead, and he may have a picture of her dead body. I feel that Andrew may have a secret or trap door somewhere in the trailer under the carpet."

Mom remembered that new carpet had recently been installed.

"I feel that Andrew may be involved with a crime gang from Tucson. He may have injured Stephanie and tried to treat her but she died from her injuries a few days later."

As she was talking to mom she indicated that she was confused because she believed that Stephanie was dead but something was telling her that she may be held captive by Andrew.

She continued, "I am going to try for better discernment on these images and tomorrow will go with a friend to Andrew's van."

Andrew was selling the van I thought was used in

Stephanie's disappearance. The medium wanted further clarity on Stephanie's whereabouts and would tell Andrew they were interested in purchasing the van.

"I will meet you in a secret location tomorrow afternoon to discuss what I learn."

Mom could not wait until the next afternoon to hear from her. If she could reveal anything new to mom, especially if it substantiated my uncle's dream, maybe the Sheriff's Office would search the van. Mom was hopeful but unfortunately Andrew cancelled the meeting.

Granny contacted the Sheriff's Office to speak with one of the Deputies but she wanted to remain anonymous. She feared Andrew's retaliation, but mom wasn't afraid of him at all. He had already ripped out her heart and taken her child. There wasn't much more he could do. Although my other children would still need my love and support, if anything happened to one of them I would be heartbroken, too. Living through a nightmare like this would be unbearable.

Mom and granny called the Sheriff's Office several times to report the leads that came their way. They seemed to have more information than the Sheriff. I don't know if any of it was ever taken seriously.

The editor of the local gossip newspaper, "The Wild West News," told granny, "A reliable source has reported that Stephanie's body is within a 35-mile radius of the tire shop Andrew owned." Granny was excited when hearing this, but when mom explained that this meant 35 miles in every direction, she became more depressed.

Granny had a special bond with Stephanie. She wasn't a grandma who baked cookies with us but she took care of us when mom needed her. Maybe granny felt guilty for not participating more in our childhood and after Stephanie's death she tried to make up for it. She always seemed to favor Stephanie when I was younger, and that bothered me. During the investigation, I felt that granny wished it was me who was missing instead of Stephanie. I realized after granny passed that she wasn't affectionate toward me because we were so much alike. We were both ambitious but the difference is that I followed my dreams and she did not. She let life get in the way and that resulted in jealousy.

She is with me in spirit today along with Stephanie. Mom and Stephanie could relate to her better than I could and I accept that, knowing that everything in our lives is intended for our good. I am now choosing to hold that recognition in love.

Roger told mom the bowling alley received a call from someone claiming to be an employee of the newspaper, saying the missing posters could be taken down because Stephanie had been found. The employee who received the call knew our family, and wanted to verify the information with Roger. He told him that she had not been found and the posters needed to stay up. We never knew the caller's identity, but mom suspected it was the EMT who said he found Stephanie in a well. This was proof that my immediate family needed to be kept out of the public eye. The tipster may not have disclosed this if he knew we were close relatives of Stephanie's and my then-husband had contacts at the bowling alley.

Mom continued to receive leads about Stephanie and September 20 was no exception. A woman called in the early morning and said, "I am not a psychic and never have strange dreams. However, I had a dream about Stephanie and wanted to tell you. I saw Stephanie wrapped in clear plastic and buried in a trench close to Andrew's property." She certainly did not hold back, and after the call ended mom stood with her arms at her side and head down reliving the conversation.

The woman should have relayed this to the Sheriff, but the small-town residents knew he would not investigate. Mom didn't want to hear the grisly details but she also didn't want to miss anything that may prove helpful.

Imagine strangers continually calling and saying hurtful things about your missing child. It was heartbreaking and painful, but we still hoped the truth would eventually be told.

At the next Board of Supervisors meeting, mom begged for a full-scale investigation. It had been 33 days since Stephanie's disappearance and our request for the Department of Public of Safety and/or the FBI to assist the Sheriff had been ignored.

She asked that the Board bring in the Department of Public Safety and/or hire a private firm to investigate, and make funds available for a more intensive search. The investigator for the Sheriff's Office briefed those who were present, about 20 relatives and residents. Many of us felt that the Sheriff wasn't doing enough but had showed up to offer support.

A representative of the Board stated, "The Sheriff has a budget and other funding sources available and the authority to request the Department of Public Safety become involved in this or any case. This committee has not been informed of any reason why this has not been done."

The committee decided that they would formally petition the Sheriff to contact the Department of Public Safety. The Board asked the County Attorney if they could offer a reward for any information leading to an arrest in the case.

The investigator for the Sheriff's Office was there to represent the Sheriff's Office. It was noted that approximately 80 hours were spent on Stephanie's case. In comparison, several hundreds of hours were spent on efforts to find a lost boy who was an out-of-state resident. Of course, we were glad that he was found. But Stephanie had been missing for a month and the Sherif had invested less than one hundred hours.

The Board of Supervisors along with the County Attorney agreed that the Board should offer a $5,000.00 reward. Both County entities agreed to write the Sheriff a letter strongly suggesting that he request help from the Department of Public Safety.

It was rumored that Andrew was connected to the Sheriff's Office as a drug informant and later that rumor was verified by a memorandum obtained by an employee of the Sheriff's Office.

Another rumor mom heard was that Andrew was receiving drugs from Tucson in tires he purchased for his business. Once the drugs arrived at his shop, they were distributed to people in town and then Andrew would notify the Sheriff's Office so they could conduct drug busts. Mom heard that Andrew was going to receive a load of tires with drugs either on September 20 or September 21. Mom informed the Sheriff in the hopes that his arrest for this would result in a conviction, since Stephanie's disappearance remained unsolved.

September 21, 1993 (Missing 34 days)

Mom called the Undersheriff after she heard that the load of tires was received at Andrew's shop. She explained that the individual watching Andrew failed to notice this shipment. No action was ever taken. This was another indication that the Sheriff's Department was protecting Andrew.

Stephanie's case was again put on the backburner because a shooting occurred involving two teenage boys. It was an afterschool fight that resulted in one teen killing another. This was an important case, but the City of Safford and their law enforcement team had jurisdiction and the Sheriff's Office had less involvement. The teen shooting was eventually solved, yet it took time away from my sister's case.

On this same day, another boy disappeared on the mountain. The lost child overshadowed Stephanie's investigation. The Sheriff's Office put all of their resources into finding him, which proved resources were available, it just depended on whether the Sheriff wanted to utilize them. In our case, he didn't.

The Undersheriff assured our family that despite these other concerns, monitoring Andrew at his shop was still a priority. If the Sheriff had requested additional manpower from the other agencies, Andrew's surveillance would have been more consistent.

September 22, 1993 (Missing 35 days)

Andrew moved out of the mobile home on the property of his tire shop and purchased a new mobile home on that site.

Every day as mom drove into town she had to pass by as it was right off the highway. I can only imagine the evidence that may have been in that mobile home.

It was the same with his van. His van was reportedly at his friend's house a week before it was sold, with the doors open as if to air it out. We thought Stephanie's body had been transported in that vehicle after her death.

These incidents were witnessed by our family and others who contacted mom. This information was passed on to the Sheriff's Office. The investigator for the Sheriff's Office claimed that he went out to see the van but didn't find anything suspicious. My intuition suggested that the van had something to do with the transportation of her body. This same van appeared in my uncle's dream.

As the last person to see her alive, Andrew should not have been able to destroy so much potential evidence. Every inch of his property should have been searched. At least the carpet of the mobile home and the van should have been tested. We were told by the Sheriff that such investigative techniques, "only happen on television."

On day 35, mom called the Undersheriff to ask how Andrew could afford a new trailer. It was obvious his tire shop was not making much money with only a few customers. If the shop was central to the drug distribution, that would explain his money. She learned Andrew had bought some land west of town.

Mom was following every lead, but it was taking a toll on her health. She was prescribed anxiety medication and had started smoking to calm her nerves.

She again contacted the Sheriff's Office saying Andrew was destroying evidence. Mom told him that she wanted the shoes she believed Stephanie was wearing that night to be tested since the psychic had recently returned them. Mom remembered Stephanie's sandals being damp when she received them from Andrew. Why did he get them wet? I do not recall rain during those two months she was missing.

The Undersheriff told her, "Norma, you need to stop feeling guilty about Stephanie's disappearance. She was an adult and lived her life the way she chose. If he isn't caught in this world and punished, he will be in the next life."

She was stunned. That a Law Enforcement Officer would say this about a suspect was troubling. We wondered if this was how he dealt with all the criminals in our town, just left it to the next life to punish them.

Mom vowed to continue her search for my sister. My family supported her since we wanted Stephanie found, or at least her body recovered.

Mom met with news organizations from Tucson and Phoenix in the city park, right across the street from the Sheriff's Office. Deputies would stand in the parking lot watching the televised reports.

Granny, mom and I were going to drive back out to where Stephanie was last seen to comb the area. We knew it was unlikely we'd find anything but we had to do something.

We were just leaving when mom received a phone call from Andrew. I could hear his voice coming through the phone and based on his tone, I could imagine his face crimson with anger. "Do you have a problem with me moving the trailer? I know your mom made a complaint."

Granny had not made a complaint and she had been

with me that day. The only other person with this knowledge was the Sheriff's employee who had been staked out watching Andrew. Mom had told him about Andrew's new mobile home. Once again, the Sheriff's office appeared to be in collusion with Andrew by feeding him this information. He should have been the prime suspect and concerns expressed by anyone, especially mom, should have remained confidential.

Mom didn't answer but he continued, "Is the psychic from Ohio planning on visiting you here in town?"

Mom explained, "She is interested in meeting with our family. However, her funds are low. If she travels out to California she may stop here, but it isn't definite."

Mom continued, "She doesn't trust the Sheriff's Office so she hasn't worked with us."

She added, "In another case she was able to locate a missing body after walking ten miles."

Anytime Andrew would hear this psychic's name he became jumpy.

"If she is coming I would like to know the timeframe," Andrew insisted.

September 23, 1993 (Missing 36 days)

Mom told Stephanie's attorney, Mariah, that she was hiring a private investigator. Mariah agreed that it was the right decision. Mariah believed there was a cover-up but couldn't determine what law enforcement was concealing. She had recently requested the petition for conservatorship and a court date was pending. The only person who might dispute this would be Andrew.

We were raising funds for a new private investigator based in Mesa, Arizona.

September 24, 1993 (Missing 37 days)

Our major fundraiser was a dance and silent auction. We received donations for the silent auction and were grateful for the support.

I was suddenly nauseated, my chest began to tighten, and I felt a sense of hopelessness. A woman helping us decorate then announced that Andrew may have taken out a large life insurance policy on Stephanie. If accurate, this provided a motive for Andrew to murder her. My intuition was again at work.

People wanted to help but this only added to our many unanswered questions. Mom wasn't sure who to believe and where to turn.

Another source confirmed that Andrew owned a .357 magnum with dual cylinders and had recently received $20,000.00. The informants did not want to speak to the Sheriff's Office and did not want their identity disclosed. They feared Andrew and considered him a threat to their lives.

Mom was exhausted from the phone calls and the gossip. She was frustrated that people would not speak directly to the Sheriff's Office, and she was hurt by what they said about her daughter.

Another report that Stephanie's body was found came over the police scanner. Someone who worked with mom heard that Stephanie had been found on Heckle Road. This had been repeated so many times we wondered if there was some truth to it. Was her body recovered and kept from the public by the Sheriff's department until they were ready to disclose the information?

We were grateful that a fresh pair of eyes would be considering the investigation. We commissioned the new private investigator and his assistant who came to Safford.

The investigator told us that he had assisted other investigators with similar unexplained cases and other drug cases in our county. These involved the same Sheriff assigned to Stephanie. My sister's case was just a small part of the corruption around this Sheriff.

The private investigator reviewed the reports and the journals mom kept since the first day of Stephanie's disappearance. Her journals included not only the evidence she had discovered but also listed all those she had contacted for help. She had separate binders for the documentation, reports, and responses to her letters from other agencies.

The investigator was impressed with her documentation. He asked mom if anyone in our family had been contacted by spirit. When mom told him that I had, he validated my encounters with my sister.

The investigator explained that there are three parts to a human being, the mind, the body, and the soul. All three must be gone for an individual to be truly dead. In my sister's case, her mind and body were taken so quickly that her spirit was confused. Thus, she reached out to us for help. This confirmed my belief that my sister was trying to communicate.

The investigator and his assistant drove out to Heckle Road. Buzzards and crows had gathered around the abandoned corrals, water troughs, and a shack with a windmill. The carcasses of a javelina and a fox had been scavenged by animals. They were only there a short time and were disemboweled and dismembered. Before the investigator arrived, mom had been back out at Heckle Road and had not seen these animals.

Our private investigators asked Andrew to meet with them and make a brief statement. Andrew said he was willing to help in any way he could. During the meeting, he said, "I feel that Norma is mistreating me. Norma didn't know that Stephanie and I were trying to work things out. I am in love with her."

He added, "During our vacation Stephanie wrote bad checks drawn from Raymond's account."

He then switched gears and talked about Stephanie's drug habit. "During our vacation, Stephanie used illegal substances and when we returned and she was arrested, I know she wasn't on drugs. Once she was released and at my house I left for a couple of hours and when I returned, she was high."

He claimed that after she was released from jail, she continued to drink and abuse drugs but hid it from others.

Those statements were contradictory. If it was difficult to tell that she was on drugs because she hid it, then how could he be certain she wasn't using on their vacation? Our family couldn't understand why the Sheriff's office with their extensive training did not recognize these inconsistencies. This was yet another indication of their negligence.

Andrew told the investigator exactly what he told the Sheriff's Office regarding the events of that night/early morning. He added that she claimed he had put a substance in his drink and she wanted some in hers. The private investigator didn't seem concerned with that statement since it wasn't originally reported.

The private investigator asked him to explain the lights going out on the truck. He stated, "About a month before the vacation, an employee of mine used the trailer to pull equipment from Phoenix to Safford. During that time a dimmer switch burned out and he replaced it. Because it wasn't done right, the lights went out."

He then described what Stephanie was wearing the day she disappeared. In past interviews with the Sheriff's Office, he didn't remember what she was wearing, only that she wore black high tops.

He told the investigator that when she was 12 she had run away from home and had returned when she was 14 years old. When she was gone, she had been involved with child pornography. This was the first time we had heard this. We aren't sure if it was true, if Stephanie made it up, or if he made it up.

Now we would direct all tips and clues from the public to the investigator, including any findings or rumors given to mom.

September 27, 1993 (Missing 40 days)

Mom contacted the investigator's office and spoke to the assistant. She explained that the Sheriff asked her to stop by his office and when she did, the Sheriff scolded her like she was a child. He expressed his disapproval of her letters to the Department of Public Safety, the Board of Supervisors, and the Attorney General's Office. Instead, the

Sheriff promised to dedicate a week of his own time to Stephanie's case.

The Sheriff was unhappy that mom had hired a private investigator and her public statements that he was not doing his job.

Andrew also claimed that Stephanie was addicted to heroin. That seemed ridiculous to us, as someone addicted to heroin needs the drug to function. Stephanie could not have been drug-free on their trip if she was addicted to heroin.

September 28, 1993 (Missing 41 days)

This investigator scheduled a briefing with his assistants. They planned an on-site search of the area where Andrew last reported seeing Stephanie on Heckle Road.

They decided to rent four-wheel all-terrain vehicles to navigate the Arizona desert. This search would take place the next day.

The following morning, they started at 8:00 a.m. The operation took nine hours to complete. Zones were divided by spiral, grid, and double-grid designations. None of these techniques were implemented by the Sheriff's Office.

The search began where Andrew reported Stephanie having exited the truck. An identifying marker there was a pile of river rock mom had stacked alongside the road. It took hours to cover the hills, valleys, and arroyos (the wash), with desert shrub, trees, and brush. The area extended four miles in each direction and the only findings were tire marks and footprints along the dirt pathways.

The results were a tattered blue towel found three

miles south of the starting point. During the search, ten coyotes were observed in the area; however, no buzzards or crows were seen. No odor of decaying flesh was detected.

October 4, 1993 (Missing 47 days)

The Sheriff and the investigator met for a three-hour lunch to discuss Stephanie's case. The Sheriff presented a receipt from the convenience store the night Andrew said he was there with Stephanie. It included the date and time along with the items purchased. This wasn't proof that Stephanie was with him. It only proved that Andrew had a receipt of what was bought at that date and time.

The Sheriff gave the investigator a report on his interview with Andrew on October 4 between 2:00 pm and 4:00 pm. However, the Sheriff was with our private investigator on that same date and time. Dates and times must be accurate in a missing persons case, and those errors pointed to his incompetency.

October 8, 1993 (Missing 51 days)

Mom met with the investigators to discuss Andrew's convictions for assault on Stephanie. Andrew had entered a treatment center outside of town for alcohol and drug addiction. Mom and the investigator wanted to substantiate this, and his accompanying record. These documents would prove that Stephanie and Andrew had a violent past and that Andrew had used drugs and alcohol.

October 9, 1993 (Missing 52 days)

The Sheriff tried to reach the investigator Saturday at 9:00

am, but no one was in the office so he left a message. This was before cell phones were in common use.

Per the message, Stephanie had been sighted at a bar in Tucson and assistance was needed on surveillance. The Sheriff had assigned deputies and he left his pager number for the investigator.

About 40 minutes later, he left another message on the answering machine. The Sheriff indicated that one of his officers had shown a picture of Stephanie to a bar patron, and that man recognized her. He said, "If that isn't the girl, then she must have a twin sister."

A deputy called mom the same day to say, "I am going to work undercover in Tucson. Is there a way to signal Stephanie? We are concerned that she might be afraid to identify herself."

Mom replied, "When my girls were young, we played a game when crossing the street." The memory brought tears.

"I would take their hands, one girl on each side. I squeezed seven times, for I-love-you-do-you-love-me, then each of my girls would squeeze back for yes."

We thought this would indicate to Stephanie that these men were working with mom. It was a glimmer of hope that she was alive.

However, the officer said to be in Tucson was spending the day at our county fair. I was at the fair that day and saw him. In fact, I saw him twice, at 6:00 p.m. and again at 11:00 p.m. I called mom to tell her.

We weren't sure if they lied about her being seen there or if it was a misunderstanding over who was assigned to Tucson. We already had reservations concerning the

Sheriff's honesty and this only compounded our fears.

Mom had hoped this would be a break in the case The betrayal she felt was heartbreaking. She had shared a memory of her daughters and they exploited it. I did not know how much more we could bear. They couldn't hide behind the lies and half-truths much longer.

October 10, 1993 (Missing 53 days)

The rumors were not much different on this day. Mom was told the Sheriff was overheard discussing the case with Andrew at a convenience store. If this was true, why would sensitive information be reviewed in public? And why would the County Sheriff be sharing it with the last person to see her alive?

October 12, 1993 (Missing 55 days)

The Sheriff told the private investigator a truck driver reported seeing Stephanie at Elmer's Bar, a topless bar, on the east side of Tucson. The Sheriff was in contact with a detective for Pima County on the fugitive detail. When we heard this, we hoped yet again that she'd be found. The episodes I had of being watched by a spirit were increasing. This uneasiness had me convinced something big was going to happen. We wanted this craziness to end as stories of the Sheriff's corruption were escalating. We couldn't understand why the Sheriff would work with Pima County, but not the Department of Public Safety.

According to the reports, Stephanie was seen with a big guy who owned a brown station wagon with an out-of-state license plate. They were said to be playing pool in the afternoon hours. Mom and I did not believe this wild tale, but still could not discount it.

The investigator's assistant asked the Sheriff to obtain the phone records for Andrew. He was one of the few people who had a cell phone at that time. The records would show any calls made from the area and to whom, on the night of Stephanie's disappearance. Andrew was known to carry his phone everywhere.

The Sheriff said the County Attorney was out of town and his approval was needed to obtain the phone records. We were incredulous that the Sheriff had not tried to access the phone records before now.

All of this increased my distress and I found it difficult to catch my breath. We were on a wild ride of emotion. The stories we heard that she had been seen in various establishments in the Tucson area brought hope followed by yet more disappointment. It was ridiculous to think that these stories might be true, yet they continued. We knew that she wasn't in these locations. Yet, we still believed, how could we not. After all this time, she would have called by now if she was alive.

MISTY PROFFITT-THOMPSON

CHAPTER SEVEN
Saying Goodbye

The private investigators drove out to Safford on October 13th to meet with mom and me. They told us that the day before, in the afternoon, a body believed to be Stephanie's was found in the desert near the San Simon wash area. We had already heard the news.

I was taking an evening college class at our local community college and on October 12, the Undersheriff came to the classroom and asked to speak to the instructor. I knew why he was there, I felt it. My instructor was surprised that a student in his class was involved in the case. We had just discussed it in his Psychology class.

My instructor approached my desk with a serious look on his face. He explained that a member of the Sheriff's Department wanted to speak with me. He advised me to take my books as I would not be returning. The room was eerily quiet and I felt blindsided. I realized that I needed to get up and leave.

I wanted to hear that Stephanie's body had been found, but on the other hand I wasn't ready to accept her death. Could I maintain my composure or would I panic? I wasn't prepared to say goodbye.

I had been expecting this for 55 days and this was the day it would end. When her story was presented in class, I hadn't admitted that it was my sister. I was embarrassed and didn't want to be judged by her behavior. At the same time, I feared breaking down and didn't want to expose my raw emotion.

The Sheriff's representative explained that a body was found and they were confident it was Stephanie. I was instructed to go to mom's house to console her. The trip to mom's was unnerving. I sensed Stephanie in the back seat of the car. I could see her in my rear-view mirror. I have since learned that transitioned souls often appear to loved ones. I believe now she was there to comfort me.

Once I arrived at mom's she was doing what I thought she would, distracting herself. We had been waiting for this moment since Stephanie was reported missing. The outcome could have been better, she could have come home alive. But here we were, and mom was busy with housework. She wanted the house clean and ready for the meals family would bring. It was going to be a long night.

The Medical Examiner was called to the scene and the body was transported to Tucson for an autopsy the next day. The Sheriff had taken her dental records to the autopsy so the body could be identified. I believe that the Sheriff knew it was Stephanie.

Mom and I found it strange that the Sheriff was present with the body for the autopsy. We weren't sure why he had this sudden interest, he hadn't shown much interest for the last 55 days. Did he attend every autopsy in Graham County?

The body was identified as Stephanie's later in the week. Mom and I were grateful that we now had closure. It may seem strange, but we knew she was free of pain. Even though her lifestyle was less than perfect, I knew she was with God.

I have been asked through the years if I believe she is in heaven. Some of the those who asked this question attended church regularly and I didn't understand that disbelief. My answer was, "Without a doubt I know that she is with God. Her human cover was battered; however, her soul is beautiful. God is the only judge, and he alone determines who enters heaven." God knew her struggles and he knows her soul.

The confirmation of her death validated that her spirit did contact me; it WAS real. I was relieved yet I was numb. At that time, I didn't know much about the transition of the soul from this realm to the next. I was determined to learn more about the spirit world.

Her body was found by two men, one of whom was affiliated with the Graham County Search and Rescue Team. The other man was the brother-in-law of one of the Deputies. The Deputy was the same officer who took the initial report from mom and Andrew. When mom asked for that report, she was told that it was lost. These details were too coincidental. I know this is a small town, but considering the number of discrepancies, it is disconcerting.

The Sheriff's actions were too suspicious. I think he knew that Stephanie's body was going to be recovered around this time and he was circulating the ridiculous stories of sightings in Tucson. I believe that our investigation put pressure on him to recover her body, instead of her being lost forever. We may never know how Stephanie died, and after all this time, I am at peace with that.

When the body was found, two Sheriff Deputies reporting to the scene was unusual, because one was always stationed elsewhere in the county.

The Department of Public Safety Crime Lab personnel and the Federal Bureau of Investigation Crime Lab personnel arrived at the scene the next morning. The investigators believe the FBI were called in because the San Simon wash area is Federal BLM land.

Our family did not receive any notification from the FBI. We hoped they were there to investigate her murder; however, they had only come to process the crime scene.

It's hard to imagine the condition of the body. The body was found with only torn gray sweatpants, on her or nearby. (The reports at the time were conflicting.) No other clothing was present on the body. A pair of Spalding black tennis shoes (investigators were told that the shoes were size 8) were located several feet from the body. They were together as if positioned afterward, with the left shoe on the left and the right shoe on the right. They were placed in a small depression on the ground.

Her left arm was torn from her body as if animals had scavenged it, found a short distance away. Excessive body fluids saturated the ground. This explained the feeling I had in the shower of my left arm tingling up and down.

The Undersheriff came to mom's house to ask if she could identify the black high tops. "I cannot be sure if those are hers, but they are similar," mom said.

He replied, "These are the shoes that were found fairly close to the body—I guess Stephanie was torn up pretty good."

Mom refused to respond to the insensitive remark.

The private investigators believed that they were lied to by the Sheriff's office. They were shown those black high top shoes in November, but that led them to question the shoes found at the scene. We wondered if they were the same pair and had been placed at the scene.

The investigators clearly remembered when they asked to examine the shoes that the deputies had needed time to find them. Those shoes should have been tagged and bagged as evidence. The investigators doubted that the tennis shoes were taken to Tucson to be analyzed as was stated in the report.

She was found at the site of a recent party. Every weekend, high schoolers and college students gathered at that desert location. It was estimated that the last event occurred one week before her body was found. Due to the decomposition of the body, those present would have smelled the odor and it would have remained with them for weeks. In fact, it has been over 20 years since I was first exposed to that smell, and I can still recall it vividly.

My step-dad went to the scene where the body was discovered and he believed it was Stephanie's. While he was there, he witnessed two DPS Crime lab technicians. He asked what they were doing, and was told they were taking soil samples.

Mom was informed by the Sheriff's secretary that prior to the positive identification of the body, the Sheriff believed it was Stephanie's because of a tattoo on the stomach area. How did the Sheriff know she had tattoos, especially a tattoo on her stomach?

This tattoo was recent and was not listed on the missing posters nor the NCIC. If it was now relevant and the sheriff had knowledge of it, why wasn't it included on any of the missing person's fliers?

The Assistant Manager of the convenience store had notified mom of the surveillance tape. The Sheriff had taken the tape for evidence and then had returned it, but the Assistant Manager noticed it was damaged. When mom had borrowed the tape prior to the Sheriff's review, it was in good condition.

Mom also told the investigators that she had the names of people who had been in the area where Stephanie's body was found. Three weeks prior to the discovery of the body, they had been collecting aluminum cans and "had covered the area pretty well." One woman said that they had scoured the ground because she had collected over one hundred cans from that outing. There were also hunters in the general vicinity of where her body had been found.

A meeting was held with the Sheriff who said he suspected Andrew was responsible for Stephanie's disappearance and now believed Andrew was responsible for her death. The Sheriff told the investigators that Stephanie's body had been recovered at approximately 2:00 p.m. on Tuesday, October 12.

The hearing on October 14 with the Superior Court Judge was to designate mom as the conservator for Stephanie. Andrew was in attendance and voiced no objections. Andrew had no rights in the matter, as they were divorced. He stated in court that money was owed by Stephanie for work on her truck. When I heard this I couldn't help but cover my face to hide the tears. Stephanie was gone and he only cared about the money. Thank goodness, the judge decided this hearing was solely for the conservatorship, and the bill would be considered at a future date.

Mom brought the order, along with a tow truck and a Deputy, to Andrew's shop to take possession of the truck. The Safford City Police Chief also accompanied them. Andrew still refused to turn the truck over to mom and the authorities. The Deputy contacted a Sheriff's Officer for instructions. The Undersheriff told him that the judge did not specify the truck, therefore mom could not take it. My tears of frustration now became tears of anger. I didn't realize that a conservatorship must itemize all property. The truck was Stephanie's and Andrew claimed he worked on it, but it didn't run. It was hard to understand why he wouldn't just hand it over. It was an attempt to further torment mom and our family.

Mom brought the issue to Stephanie's attorney. Together they petitioned the judge who granted the conservatorship. His response was patronizing and he simply passed the request on to the County Attorney's Office. After their plea was repeated to the County Attorney, he promised to address it, but did nothing.

October 19, 1993

The private investigators came to Safford and spoke with one of Andrew's ex-girlfriends. She was a cousin to us through marriage. She began seeing Andrew in March 1989 and after three weeks moved in with him. Before she lived with him, Andrew pursued her by leaving notes and following her.

The first two months they lived together were happy, then she suspected he was cheating. Andrew began bragging to her that he was seeing one of her cousins, but didn't mention Stephanie's name. When Stephanie met this girl, they didn't recognize each other and Stephanie didn't know her cousin was pregnant with Andrew's baby. The two young women became friends.

The relationship between Andrew and his pregnant girlfriend deteriorated. Andrew started abusing her in June or late May. He locked her in the bedroom because she continued to smoke while she was pregnant. The more he drank, the worse it got. He would slap her and he also threatened her with a butcher knife. He choked her until she passed out. He chased her with a belt.

These were my sister's friends. Although I have compassion for the women Andrew abused, including my sister, they chose to stay with him. As I am writing this, my heart breaks for what she suffered. I feel her telling me that it was destined to be this way. When my soul transitions it will make more sense.

Each time I feel her presence, I know that she is okay with what she suffered. I feel her soul telling me that enough time has passed for her to accept this story being shared with the public.

That wasn't always her feeling. When she was missing, she didn't want us to know the details of her life and death. I could feel her shame.

Now I feel that she is in a much better place and she is at peace with her journey. She has come to terms with her decisions in life. As I write this, I feel a wisp of air close to my ear and I look up and see that the time is 8:18 pm. That time always resonates with me as she was declared missing on August 18. She is with me now. She is validating the telling of our story.

Another ex-girlfriend of Andrew's had experiences like Stephanie's. She told the investigator she was with him for about four or five months back in the mid-1980s. She said that he beat her and had shot her up with crystal meth while she slept and that he put rat poison in her drink. He used drugs and she thought they were supplied by someone in Phoenix. She confirmed that Andrew was an informant for at least two police investigators.

Since the investigators were present for that interview, Andrew's polygraph examination was discussed. Discrepancies were found in the polygraph.

October 20, 1993

This was the day of her funeral. On one hand, we were glad to at least have closure. On the other hand, we had to accept her death. My dad drove down from California for the funeral. He is not good at processing emotion so I know this was difficult for him. But it was difficult for all of us.

He blamed himself and still does, and so does my mom. The difference between mom and dad is that mom fights back where my dad runs, but neither is right or wrong. If I were in that situation, I would do a little of both, but everyone grieves in their own way.

The investigators received a phone call from the attorney. Mom had filed an order of protection against Andrew for our family because of his prior assault charges and his intimidation and aggression toward us. By his own admission, he left her out in the desert alone. Because this was signed by a judge on October 20, he could not attend her funeral with us. I believe he had no remorse for his part in Stephanie's death and only wanted to be there to play mind games.

The funeral was a closed casket and the funeral home was packed with mourners. My oldest daughter, then seven, was teary-eyed, but insisted on attending the funeral. My boys were too young to go so they stayed with the sitter. I remember seeing people there from my work, which brought me comfort.

The funeral director had asked if we wanted to decorate and display a felt board for the funeral. This was an opportunity to honor Stephanie's memory through pictures of happier times.

I was filled with sorrow as we were driven to the cemetery. The Sheriff of all people led the procession. We were desperate for answers and I had such contempt for him that I didn't speak to him the entire day, it wasn't the time nor the place. Maybe he wanted to lead us to ease his guilt. I haven't lost much sleep over that.

After the funeral, we headed to mom's house. I was so sick I couldn't eat. I not only felt my sorrow but also the grief, anger, and frustration of our family and friends. I have since learned to shield myself from others' emotions.

My job was supportive and offered me as much time off as I needed. I stayed home the day after the body was found until three days after the funeral. Roger gave me a hard time for being with mom every day. After the funeral he said, "She's gone, so get over it."

I understand now that he had his own pain, and his anger wasn't directed at me. But at the time, when I heard that, I lost it. Mom gave me half a tranquilizer and when I woke up it was dark and everyone had left.

7 | SAYING GOODBYE

The day after the funeral mom called the private investigators and told them she had spoken to the Sheriff. After the service, he asked mom to stop by his office. She brought me along.

"Norma and Misty, it is great to see you," the Sheriff began. "I'd like to address a few items with you." We both hoped he would tell us about how she died now that her body had been found and positively identified.

"First, I would like for you to make a list of all the strange things that Andrew has done. Second, I want to know if you have changed your mind about going to New York and appearing on that talk show to discuss Stephanie's case. My wife and I would love to see New York, and Andrew said he wanted to go, too."

The day after my sister's funeral was not the time to discuss vacation plans. Mom didn't think this was appropriate, especially since the investigation was still ongoing. Mom had noticed Andrew's odd behavior from the beginning and the Sheriff had done nothing about it, so why now?

October 22, 1993

Mom met with the County Attorney. He stated that because her body was now identified there would be a further investigation and the Department of Public Safety would be assisting.

The County Attorney seemed surprised when mom told him that the Sheriff's Office said they would be investigating and that the Department of Public Safety would only send lab crews. She was told this when she called the DPS Office to speak with the Officer-In-Charge of Stephanie's investigation.

She asked the County Attorney why Andrew's van, his other vehicles, trailer and property had not been searched or tested by DPS. The County Attorney seemed surprised at hearing this, too. He said he would advise the Sheriff that these procedures should be carried out.

He then asked if mom would submit her journals to him for his review. Mom didn't feel comfortable parting with them, so she refused. She had already told him what was in her journals and he didn't believe her. Was he planning to confiscate them?

Raymond called to say that Andrew had rented an apartment in Morenci after Stephanie's disappearance and he may have kept Stephanie's dogs there. Andrew had an aunt who lived in Morenci. Coincidently on this same date, the owner of our small-town gossip paper notified granny that Andrew's grandmother told him Stephanie's dogs were locked up in an apartment in Morenci. She said Andrew's aunt who lived in Morenci was feeding them. We learned later that these dogs had attacked Andrew and he killed them.

October 23, 1993

Granny received a phone call from a Graham County Deputy who did not identify himself. He said the Deputies wanted to tell our family they were sorry for our loss and that a better investigation should have been conducted.

October 24, 1993

Mom received a phone call from a woman who stated that

Andrew had asked her father-in-law to notarize documents. The contents were not identified since this notary did not keep a log; however, she said Andrew was signing Stephanie's name. Andrew told the notary that he had the Power of Attorney. Andrew had been going to this notary for three weeks prior to this date. We considered this unprofessional and unethical. The power of attorney authorizes someone to sign their name in the place of the name they represent, with the power of attorney attached, not to sign the other person's name. This man was negligent in his duties as a notary.

Mom was able to reach him after several attempts to verify this. He admitted to notarizing documents for Andrew that concerned Stephanie's legal work and said he would not do business with Andrew again. He could not recall what he had notarized.

October 25, 1993

Mom told the private investigators that a Deputy contacted granny and would not identify himself. He claimed to have overheard the Sheriff saying he planned to kill granny.

Mom witnessed Andrew moving his van into one of his shop stalls and cleaning it. Mom contacted the primary private investigator about preserving evidence that may be in the van, or at least conducting a search of the vehicle before Andrew could destroy the evidence.

We found it difficult to believe that the van had not been searched, nor any of his other property. The investigator told her to contact the County Attorney.

Mom went to the County Attorney's office. "Andrew has sold the van and the person who bought it returned it.

When I saw Andrew, he was cleaning the van," mom explained to the County Attorney.

"I am not an investigator, nor am I responsible for this investigation. I will talk to the Sheriff to see if he has probable cause for seizing the van. It was my understanding that Andrew was driving his truck the night Stephanie disappeared."

Mom answered, "You are right, but two witnesses saw Andrew driving the van at 5:30 a.m. on the morning of August 18. Andrew admitted to going back to pick up the van when the lights went out on the truck."

I am still not convinced of the story he told about the lights. In our area, the sun would have come up around 5:00 to 5:30 a.m. on that date. Why would he drive his truck back to his house without lights and leave her out there alone? I am convinced that his story is false.

"Cleaning the van does sound suspicious and I will double-check with the Sheriff to see if the van can be seized to prevent Andrew from disposing of any possible evidence," the County Attorney assured mom.

"By the way, I still would like a copy of your journals," he added.

No action by the County Attorney was ever taken.

October 28, 1993

The investigators received many phone calls after the body was found. One was from Raymond stating he witnessed the Sheriff and three Deputies at Andrew's shop. The Deputies went into the shop and were there for around fifteen minutes. During that time, Andrew was not present

7 | SAYING GOODBYE

at the shop. In fact, he wasn't even in Safford.

I am sure Andrew regretted having a shop positioned right off the main highway. Everyone who lived south of town drove that road as there was no other way to reach their homes.

The investigators received information that not only was the Sheriff at Stephanie's autopsy, but he had invited the entire Search and Rescue Team from Graham County to be present. We felt as though Stephanie had been degraded and exploited.

Stephanie wasn't there. Her body was only a shell for my sister's soul during her 23 years here and nothing more. Her beautiful spirit left that battered body and was in the most amazing place...Heaven. It didn't matter that the Sheriff wanted to feed his ego by making a spectacle of her remains.

I find it difficult to believe that the volunteers of the Graham County Search & Rescue Team view all autopsies of unexplained deaths in our small community.

The investigators received a phone call on October 30 from a reporter at the Eastern Arizona Courier. He stated that he had been to the scene where Stephanie's body was recovered prior to its being sealed.

This reporter had pictures of the crime scene and was willing to share them with the private investigators. The investigators could retrieve the pictures when they came back to Safford on a subsequent trip. We are not sure if the Sheriff's Office received the same photos.

On the same day, granny voiced her concerns to the Chairman of the Graham County Board of Supervisors.

"I cannot understand why the Sheriff has been treating

us with such disrespect. Our family has never been involved with anything like this, so we were unsure of the protocol. If the Sheriff had any people skills, he would have understood our concerns and worked with us instead of against us.

"We also found it unusual that the Sheriff and Andrew have been seen numerous times talking in a friendly manner."

The Chairman explained, "I believe the Sheriff was somehow involved with her murder. That is why he acted unprofessionally."

CHAPTER EIGHT
Believing the Unbelievable

At the first of November, the private investigators learned Andrew had an apartment in the Clifton area, close to Duncan and about the same distance from Safford. These leads were pursued because of a comment by one of the Deputies that indicated Stephanie had been traveling to Duncan sometime in the weeks prior to her disappearance. Duncan, Morenci, and Clifton are all near one another. They also wanted to verify that Andrew owned an apartment in the Morenci area.

It now seemed possible that Andrew may have taken Stephanie to the Duncan area against her will prior to her death. In an interview with the investigators, one of Andrew's ex-girlfriends said Andrew had held her against her will during their relationship.

Mom went to court for the hearing on the order of protection. This order was approved temporarily the day of the funeral until a formal hearing could be scheduled. The hearing was to determine if the order of protection was warranted.

During the inquiry, the discrepancies in Andrew's story were noticeable. He was under oath during the hearing, yet he still lied. He again stated that he never assaulted Stephanie. He stated that he did not carry a weapon as it was a condition of his probation that he not possess a weapon. Several people could verify that he did in fact display his handgun.

When asked if he ever had Stephanie's signature notarized prior to her death or during her disappearance, he stated that he hadn't, yet there were two people present stating the opposite.

Thank goodness, the order of protection was approved. It brought us some relief to know that he could no longer contact us.

After the hearing, mom and the attorney went to the Sheriff's Office to pick up some of Stephanie's belongings Andrew had said would be there. He stated they would be in the basement of the Sheriff's Office.

When they arrived, they observed a large gray suitcase. They asked the Deputies whether this had been brought in by Andrew and they said they did not know. My mom went through the contents of the suitcase and discovered that they were Stephanie's. Mom was Stephanie's conservator yet still had not received anything from Andrew's house; at least now she could take the suitcase.

Around this time, the private investigator and his assistant returned to Safford. They met with mom and she gave them a pale mint-green and light pale-pink tie-dyed, short-sleeve t-shirt. Mom explained that this shirt was one that Andrew returned in the suitcase and it appeared to be bleached or more washed-out than she remembered. The investigators agreed that the colors appeared faded. The investigators also noticed a stain near the bottom hem in the front. Like the shirt, the stain seemed faded. There were other, dark gray spots at the bottom hem of the shirt.

The investigators were told that while dining at a local restaurant, someone overheard a Deputy saying that he did not think Stephanie's body had been at the site where it was discovered for more than three days. Furthermore, the ground beneath her body was very cold, much colder than the surrounding area. The Deputy was one of the first law enforcement officials on the scene when the body was discovered.

While in town, the investigators went to Heckle Road where the Gatorade bottle was found, now marked by a pile of river rocks. Their objective was to determine how long it would take to walk from where Andrew alleged that he had dropped Stephanie off, to the highway. The female investigator walked the distance and they estimated it would have taken Stephanie almost two hours to reach the highway.

Andrew stated during his pre-polygraph interview that he stopped at the old inspection station on the highway to work on his lights. In his words, "There is a death-to-dawn light there at that location." We believe his words, "death-to-dawn," instead of dusk-to-dawn, constituted a Freudian slip, referring to Stephanie's death.

I cannot understand why he left Stephanie out there to retrieve another vehicle. Based on his claims, the vehicle did not have working lights, so it would have been difficult to drive to his residence in the dark. The investigators went to the inspection station at night and found no security or dusk-to-dawn lights anywhere onsite. The investigators spoke to the residents in the area and they all agreed that the station had been closed for some time.

The investigators also stated that if Stephanie was out there between the hours of 4:30 to 5:30 a.m., she would have been reported. The highway Stephanie was thought to have walked was known to have heavy traffic as it was the main route for those who worked the copper mine in Morenci. The highway was busy at all hours of the day and night.

This portion of the investigation was now complete. The investigators' analysis was on to the circumstances of Stephanie's disappearance and the validity of Andrew's statements. The Sheriff's Office did not address these concerns during their investigation.

Mom gave the private investigators a written statement from a witness. It read, "Late last summer, Andrew and Stephanie were together at my house. Andrew expressed his apprehension about Raymond coming here. Andrew went to his truck and pulled out a gun. He then went in the backyard and started arguing with Stephanie. During the argument, Andrew was waving the gun at her. They left in separate vehicles."

Mom received similar stories of Stephanie's abuse during this time of grief. People did not feel comfortable reporting incidents to the Sheriff's Office for fear of retaliation, so they contacted mom. She appreciated their efforts but it was difficult to hear the rumors. She was afraid the one phone call she did not take would be the most important.

The private investigators asked the Sheriff's Office for the official file on Stephanie's case. It stated that two individuals found her body and the autopsy report gave the body weight of the remains at 31 pounds.

It had apparently been moved or dragged on two different occasions and it was speculated that the body may have been ravaged by an animal. There were two separate places where it appeared body fluid drained from the body, one large spot and another smaller area some feet away. At that final location, there was little if any drainage.

There were no pictures in the Sheriff's file, only a written description. It seems that a crime scene like this with so many unanswered questions would have photos and detailed reports. The autopsy was inconclusive as to the cause of death.

In the file was the interview of an individual who claimed she last saw Stephanie on the Monday or Tuesday prior to her disappearance. The private investigators questioned why she had not been interviewed previously. This person's name was not given to the private investigators and there was no other mention of her.

There were five individuals who recalled seeing a woman walking north on Heckle Road and west on the highway in the morning hours of August 20. An investigator from the Sheriff's Office had interviewed all five sources.

The file contained an interview on August 19 with Raymond. This stated that Raymond saw Andrew and Stephanie on August 18 at 10:30 a.m. Investigators from the Sheriff's Office had searched Raymond's property but found nothing of interest.

Further documentation stated that Raymond's property was searched, but Andrew's property was not. Since Andrew admitted that he was the last person to see her alive, his property should have been considered a source of potential evidence.

That was the extent of the case file on her disappearance. The private investigator found it odd that there was no mention of Andrew's interview. The investigator did receive a notification later from the Sheriff. This listed Andrew's interview by the Sheriff as having been conducted on October 4. Based on his admissions, it was strange that the first interview was on October 4, day 47 of her disappearance. This interview was said to have occurred at the same time the investigators were having lunch with the Sheriff.

The Sheriff's Office gave the investigators conflicting reports. Mom received reports that differed from the originals.

The investigator requested copies of the files. The copies were sent three months later, February 1994. They contained no additional information.

The private investigators contacted individuals who knew Andrew and/or Stephanie. They spoke to a man who saw Andrew regularly. He worked at a gun shop and for the Graham County Animal Control.

He told the private investigator about a death that occurred when Andrew was present. Andrew and a friend rode motorcycles one night out to the hot tubs. Mom and I heard that this happened a couple of years before Stephanie met Andrew. It was reported that during the trip the friend bent down to adjust the carburetor and lost control of his motorcycle. Andrew was riding behind him and to the side on his own motorcycle. A truck driver brought the man to the hospital. It was unclear why Andrew did not accompany his injured companion. The person who relayed this to the private investigators was haunted by the similarities between this death and Stephanie's.

He verified that Andrew never left his house or business without his mobile phone. Back in the early '90s only the wealthy or certain employees carried a mobile phone. This person claimed that Andrew had not used his phone the night Stephanie disappeared. I am not sure how he would know that.

If that were true, Andrew could have used it that morning to call for help. Or he could have called mom. We wondered if she was out there with him or if that was another fabrication.

This source also said the videotape from the convenience store showed Andrew appearing to wear his mobile phone on his belt. The private investigators had viewed the video and they also thought he was wearing his mobile phone.

He continued, "I have been receiving threats from the Sheriff, like, 'Be careful you don't fall.' Because I record the scanner and listen to it while I work, the Sheriff is worried about what I might know. That's why he doesn't want me around." He seemed nervous as he spoke.

"I agreed to distribute forms to recall the Sheriff. I work out of my vehicle because the owner of the gun shop who was employed by the Sheriff's Office lost his job. An Undersheriff fired him for distributing the forms from his shop. I have received information that the Sheriff told Andrew about your investigation."

The investigator replied, "Norma hired us and this is a private inquiry, so I am not sure where that information originated."

The source continued, "The Sheriff told Andrew they are between a rock and a hard place. The Sheriff is afraid of what mom and granny might discover. Andrew and the Sheriff are together on this because Andrew was the Sheriff's informant."

The Sheriff needed Andrew's help with drug busts. Andrew gave the Sheriff the locations of drug exchanges. Now that Andrew was in trouble, the Sheriff had to protect him, otherwise Andrew might expose the Sheriff's involvement.

"I know for a fact that the Sheriff has served false search warrants on Raymond in the past," the employee said.

The conversation ended and the private investigators could substantiate the information. It didn't relate to Stephanie's death directly, but it did point to corruption involving the Sheriff.

By mid-November, mom still did not have the personal belongings Andrew had been ordered to return. The items included a gun, a throwing dagger, a Black Hills gold necklace and ring, a pair of earrings, and some ironwood turtles.

The Sheriff's Office also had some of Stephanie's property, her purse and three pairs of sandals, including the white huaraches that mom believed Stephanie was wearing the night of her disappearance.

Mom asked the Sheriff's Office if they had tested the shoes and at that time they had not. This was potential evidence recovered in a missing persons/murder investigation.

Mom obtained Stephanie's medical records from three

clinics and the hospital. She also obtained a copy of a report from the Superior Court Records on the incident between Andrew and Stephanie.

This was when he beat her with a crowbar prior to November 14, 1989. Stephanie filed a report and Andrew was arrested on November 14, but Stephanie decided not to press charges and they were dropped. Mom remembered that a report was made to the Graham County Sheriff's Office and she witnessed a Deputy and a female employee of the Sheriff's Office take photographs of Stephanie.

When Andrew was arrested, he spent between seven to ten days at the Graham County Jail and was later transferred to Maricopa County.

Mom was notified by a co-worker that the files for Raymond and Andrew were missing from the courthouse; an employee of the court records section verified that Raymond's files were missing but assumed they were at County Attorney's Office.

When the investigators checked the Graham County Superior Court Records, the only file there on Andrew was for the crowbar incident.

The private investigators spoke to mom about Andrew's past. "Andrew had several arrests, including kidnapping and possession of stolen property; however, the kidnapping charge was ultimately dropped."

Mom replied, "Stephanie disappeared for a short period in August 1992. She said she had been kidnapped and imprisoned by Andrew."

Mom was filled with remorse over this incident. At the time, she hadn't believed Stephanie. Mom thought Stephanie wanted sympathy and this was just another way to manipulate her. Mom had notified the Sheriff's Office of her disappearance and they had said she was probably on a "partying binge." Stephanie came home after three days.

When mom learned of Andrew's arrest charges, she realized Stephanie could have been kidnapped. Mom added that the Undersheriff and a Jailer offered to help when she reported Stephanie missing.

November 16, 1993

The private investigator received a phone call from the Sheriff. He said he wanted to meet in Safford the following day.

He said he asked the County Attorney to subpoena Andrew's telephone bills. The private investigator had suggested he subpoena Andrew's phone bills at an earlier time. Andrew also said he had volunteered to give the bills to the Sheriff's Office earlier but no one seemed interested.

On that same day, mom told the private investigator, "I received a phone call from the local Victim Witness Program. Their representative offered to give me the autopsy report on Stephanie."

Mom continued, "Why is the Victim Witness Program involved when the Sheriff's Office would not designate Stephanie as a victim? The local gossip paper also had the autopsy report before I did."

Mom added, "I contacted the County Attorney and he said the autopsy report was public information."

The private investigator responded, "Given the circumstances, you have a right to be angry, but let us handle this."

Mom was reluctant to follow his advice, but agreed.

We understood that her autopsy was public information; however, the Coroner's office denied mom a copy of the report since it was under investigation. Accordingly, no one should have received a copy until Stephanie's death was solved, if ever.

Because the Sheriff did not consider her a victim or her death a homicide, the family should have received the results first. It was a shock to hear that the editor of the local gossip paper was asking for it.

The investigators spoke to the Sheriff on November 17 to review the autopsy report but the Sheriff claimed it had not been released. Mom contacted the Coroner's Office and they said they had sent it to him on November 10. Mail from Tucson to Safford should take no more than three days.

When mom contacted them again, they said they sent a full report to the Graham County Attorney on November 10. The Sheriff said on November 17 he had not received it, but the local gossip paper received it before November 17.

If the County could not agree on a simple report, how could they conduct a homicide investigation? The inconsistencies continued.

During the time Stephanie was missing and after her body was found, mom never let her guard down in public. But the grief and sadness took a toll on her health.

The editor from the Wild West News received a phone call from a woman who claimed to represent the Dallas "Unsolved Mysteries." She had a picture of the Sheriff leaving a hotel in Phoenix with Stephanie. Later, the private investigators questioned the Sheriff, and he admitted to having heard that rumor, but denied any knowledge of the incident.

His involvement with Stephanie should not have shocked me. Before this nightmare began, I was told by mutual acquaintances that Andrew was escorting her. I hope this wasn't true, but anything was possible. And I knew that the Sheriff could not be trusted. He recognized the tattoo on her stomach, one mom had heard of only recently. This was just more speculation; we didn't know who or what to believe.

November 17, 1993

The private investigators were once again in town. They drove by Andrew's properties located in Safford and Thatcher. They conducted more interviews. These efforts did nothing to further the investigation.

The investigators met with the Sheriff to discuss the black high tops. Andrew repeated his story that Stephanie was wearing them to the hot tubs that night, which seemed unlikely. Since they were going to the hot tubs, it was more likely she would have worn sandals. Based on Andrew's account that she was anxious to leave, the idea that she would take the time to put socks on and then the high tops was not logical.

The Deputy who completed the original report sketched the shoe print found at the site. It doesn't make sense that pictures weren't taken of the shoe print. That is a basic procedure in every crime scene investigation. Perhaps pictures would have conflicted with the account given in the report.

The private investigators informed the Sheriff, "Based on the information, Andrew should be indicted for involuntary manslaughter."

Andrew left Stephanie out in the desert at night, aware of her physical and mental condition.

They continued, "Andrew perjured himself during the order of protection hearing when he claimed that he had never physically abused anyone, including Stephanie. Not only is there evidence that he abused Stephanie, an ex-girlfriend of Andrew's was hospitalized from his abuse."

The Sheriff's Office would not charge him with murder or involuntary manslaughter.

The girlfriend requested the police report based on the charges she filed against Andrew, but was denied for unspecified reasons.

The Sheriff responded, "I cannot substantiate those charges. The evidence is circumstantial. Too much time has passed on the charges made by Andrew's ex-girlfriend."

The investigator said, "Andrew's ex-girlfriend is currently under psychiatric care and afraid of Andrew, but she is willing to testify. If necessary, we can bring this to a grand jury."

The Sheriff answered, "The County Attorney would never agree to that."

The investigator believed Andrew's admitting to being the last person to see her alive should be sufficient motive. He wondered if our county officials were capable of performing even the most basic duties.

The investigator remembered the Sheriff had stated earlier Andrew was the main suspect in her disappearance and death.

He said, "The polygraph results found Andrew's responses inconclusive. Innocence or guilt cannot be determined without a proper investigation. Andrew has a violent criminal history, beginning when he was a teenager."

The Sheriff replied, "Raymond also has a similar history with the law. The checks she stole and cashed would give Raymond motive."

As far as we know, Raymond never held her against her will. He had been abusive, but there is no indication that he would murder her.

Some of the visions I had did include a man that fit his description, but I could not see his face. I saw Stephanie in a black wooden box that looked like a casket. A man wearing a denim shirt with the sleeves cut off was hovering above the box. This box was moved at least three times and I also saw a barrel cactus with an orange bloom. None of that proved to me that the killer was either of these men. I only received images and feelings.

The next day, the investigators wanted to question Andrew's employee. One investigator drove to Andrew's shop, but Andrew would not allow him in. It was agreed that they would speak later that night at the Sheriff's Office.

The private investigator asked the Sheriff about the items belonging to Stephanie. He wanted to see the black Spalding shoes found near Stephanie's body. The Sheriff's Department could not initially locate the shoes. Neither the shoes nor her purse had been processed as evidence. The shoes were found in a white plastic garbage bag. We were told such procedures for preserving evidence were only done in the movies.

The private investigators examined a pair of Stephanie's white sandals that mom had given to the Sheriff. She had received them from Andrew several days after her disappearance. Mom did not believe that Stephanie was wearing the black tennis shoes at the time of her disappearance. Mom made several requests for Andrew to produce them and he finally turned them over to her. I didn't see Stephanie much, but when I did, she was wearing those white sandals.

The private investigators wanted to inspect Stephanie's handbag, but were denied access by the Sheriff. He instead pulled out from her bag four checking and savings account books, old deposit stubs, and several receipts. One of the accounts had a duplicate check for a copayment to a local clinic on August 9. The Sheriff told the private investigators that he had not inspected the contents of the purse before that date. There could have been a receipt from the convenience store in her purse, a note with useful information, something that could have helped the investigation, yet the contents weren't examined by the Sheriff's Office until then.

The private investigators returned to the Sheriff's Office that night to speak with one of Andrew's employees.

He explained, "I worked in the shop on August 17 until 5:30 p.m., but stayed late to work on my own vehicle until about 9:00 p.m. That day, Andrew, Stephanie, and two friends were there. One of the friends was helping me on my car. Stephanie's truck was in the shop for a week prior to that night and Andrew was messing with it that night. I do not remember if she was drinking. Stephanie and Andrew argued more when she had been drinking."

The private investigator asked, "Did Stephanie use drugs?"

He responded, "I imagine that she did, because people have told me that. When I arrived home from the shop it was about 9:00 p.m. and I stayed up until 11:00 p.m."

The investigator said, "Do you recall if Stephanie and Andrew had been fighting that evening?"

He responded, "They fight every now and then, but I have never seen Andrew hit Stephanie. When I arrived, Stephanie and Andrew were not arguing and I was scheduled to work the following day, August 18. When I got to work at 8:00 a.m. that day, the shop was open and Andrew was there. At that time, Andrew told me that he and Stephanie were going to the hot tubs, but they had an argument."

The investigator asked, "What do you know about the lights on Andrew's truck?"

He said, "I fixed the lights. The headlight switch was out on the dash, and Andrew ordered one from a local auto parts store. We had been pulling a horse trailer and the lights had gone out a couple of times and after I put a dimmer switch in, the lights again went out. I ordered another part and once that arrived I installed it and it seemed to work fine from there."

The investigator continued, "How successful is the business for Andrew?"

The employee explained, "The most he has made in one day is about $2,000.00. When Stephanie and Andrew were on vacation, I put the day's receipts in a drawer and

Stephanie's mom would make the deposits."

***

Unfortunately, Stephanie's death was never solved. The investigators continued to work on it. Andrew's day in court for the murder of my sister never came. A court hearing was held for wrongful death because he left her out in the desert in the summer, having admitted that she was not in her right state of mind. She was not in good health and she was recovering from a foot injury. He was not found responsible.

This event was life-changing for me. I could choose to respond to evil with hate or love. It is difficult to view this experience with eyes of love, but I know it happened for a reason, one we may never know. It would be easy to give up and give in to hate.

I believe that Andrew lived a life dictated by evil. I also believe that evil preys on those who are weak by offering empty promises. Andrew chose to walk this path and Stephanie also made choices that led her down that path. While he was alive, Andrew thought he had won, but in life there is no winning or losing. We all must live with the consequences of our choices.

I chose to approach this experience with love, forgiveness, and patience. I know mom wanted to be positive, but having to live with a piece of your heart missing cannot be easy. I couldn't bear losing one of my children. I fear I would sink into a deep depression. I admire mom's strength and that she has now found her new normal and is learning to live in peace.

We continue to have unanswered questions. Mom and granny tried to keep the fight going; however, over time it just became exhausting. The recall efforts to displace the Sheriff also fizzled but when re-elections were held, he lost. The incoming Sheriff tried to do what he could for our family, but too much time had elapsed.

Andrew was sentenced to prison later on an unrelated charge. While driving to Phoenix from Safford on the State Highway, he had an incident with some young drivers on the road. That was years after Stephanie passed away. It was my understanding that he had to serve most of his time in a solitary unit for his own protection because of those at the prison he set-up and/or testified against. He was in prison for about 13 years. When released, he was out for about eight months and then died from complications of HIV and Hepatitis C.

Karma played a part in our finding justice. I believe in an afterlife and possibly in reincarnation, to correct mistakes made in life the first time on earth.

In the meantime, we are still trying to live without Stephanie. Mom struggled to get back to a routine. She believes that Stephanie is with her. I am glad mom has found comfort in her faith.

CHAPTER NINE
Focusing on My Gifts

Our family suffered a horrendous loss, yet we must move forward. I am grateful and feel privileged to have had her spirit communicate with me while her physical body was missing, yet for many years after that I had very few experiences. I was busy with work, family, and other responsibilities and my mind was not receptive. Spirit would come and lights would turn on randomly and I would hear my name spoken. I would have visions of people I could speak to, but more often I would feel their presence. Some of these events happened when I was with family members.

One night, I was sitting on my bed watching a cartoon with my then four-year-old daughter (she is now 14). My husband was working on one of our ceiling fans in the formal living room and my daughter and I heard a strong feminine voice say, "Misty."

The name was slow and drawn out. I ignored it because I didn't want to frighten my daughter. I had heard my name called in the past, so this wasn't new to me.

My daughter nudged me and asked, "Mommy, did you hear that?"

I answered, "What, Missy?" using my nickname for my daughter.

She stated, "Somebody said your name, Misty."

I assured her that I heard it, too.

My daughter ran to my husband to ask if he was calling me and he said no.

This was validation for me that angels and/or spirits are speaking to me and I am grateful that they are present with me. I am also grateful that my daughter can hear them.

I began to open up further to spirit when I received a set of Angel Oracle Cards created by Doreen Virtue. Spirit was already preparing my future and I didn't realize it.

In November 2003, mom and I went to see James Van Praagh in Scottsdale. It was the first session with a medium we had attended. Up to that point, I had seen mediums on television. I have an open mind and I believe that with God anything is possible, especially since I have experienced spiritual phenomenon. I was hoping to receive validation of our experiences with Stephanie's spirit.

The day before the event we were both nervous and hopeful. It was to be a getaway for mom and me. We left early as it was a three-hour drive; partway to Scottsdale, we stopped at a casino on the Apache Indian Reservation. We walked out $300.00 richer than we walked in. We took that as a sign that this day was going to be great.

When we arrived at the venue, we sat in a room with about 1200 people. James started by doing readings for the entire group. He stated that someone at the opposite side of the room had lost a child and it happened outside. Mom grabbed my hand and as my heart raced, he said that the person who had crossed was an adult. He said this person had a cracked skull. No one raised their hand to acknowledge this reading. Mom leaned over and whispered to me that she believed this was about Stephanie.

9 | FOCUSING ON MY GIFTS

He stated that the individual who passed on was greeted by a loved one and the family member in the audience had a name like the man who was helping her cross over. We were sure this was her spirit speaking.

Mom stood up and said that her youngest daughter, an adult who was missing for 55 days, had been found and a funeral had been held for her.

James asked if mom had another daughter in the audience with her and she said that she did, so I stood up.

He told me that I had an older female standing over me and she was my spirit guide. He said this individual was wearing an old-fashioned nurse's uniform with a cape and she was a nurse for the military.

He said my sister was there in the room with us and she wanted to thank me for helping her cross over. He explained that she was sorry for what she had done.

At that point, I started to cry. I always knew that she was with me but this confirmed it.

He told mom that she was okay and that her death was not painful.

He said that she was watching over the girl on the purple bicycle.

Specifics on her death weren't given. It was Stephanie saying, 'I am okay.'

All the way home from Scottsdale, mom and I kept repeating what we'd heard. I couldn't believe that we had a reading. It was a confirmation of Stephanie's presence and that our loved ones never leave us, they just change form. It reaffirmed all that I had experienced, and I was thankful to have received this message.

I wondered about the nurse James saw standing behind me. On the way home mom said that my great-grandmother, on my dad's side, was a nurse in World War II. I later asked my dad about her and he gave me a picture; the uniform looked exactly as James had described. It was encouraging to know that someone on the other side was watching over me besides my sister.

I also wondered who the girl was on the purple bicycle. My youngest daughter had never met Stephanie in her physical form. She did have a small bicycle with training wheels but it was pink.

My older daughter, however, had been close to Stephanie and would stay with her when my sister was not using drugs. Stephanie was liked by children, older people, and animals. I asked my daughter the color of the bicycle she had then, but did not tell her about our experience. It had been a stressful time, and I could not remember.

When she said purple, it made perfect sense. Stephanie was watching over the niece she had loved. My daughter was preparing to attend college and Stephanie would be guiding and protecting her.

After the reading from James Van Praagh, I felt more comfortable about the messages I had received from Stephanie all those years earlier. I believed I had connected with spirit.

I read the instructions more carefully on the Angel Oracle cards and started practicing card readings. I searched the internet for information on Doreen Virtue and downloaded her podcasts from Hay House. Doreen had written several books that I ordered and read. I also purchased her Angel Oracle Cards. Doreen gave classes

9 | FOCUSING ON MY GIFTS

both online and in person to become a Certified Angel Card Reader.

I was trying to find my purpose as my work was no longer satisfying. It was a great-paying government job, had great benefits, and a great retirement package; however, I didn't feel fulfilled. I was certain there had to be something more for me. Something bigger and better.

I always believed that my position would prepare me for my true calling. I took advantage of all the extra training I was offered. The seminars included supervisory training, and later in my career I was appointed to organize audits, oversee people who worked in the command center during emergencies, and organize their training. I was appointed to serve as a Public Information Officer, and I worked in that capacity for six years. I trusted my guidance and now I know that those tasks taught me the skills and abilities I use today.

I didn't know what I was called to do, but I began developing my spiritual gifts. I knew that they would become important once I retired, so I tried to learn all I could about spirit-based careers.

Some areas I excelled in and others not so much. I was being guided in the right direction, although back then I didn't trust my intuition as much as I do now.

I enrolled in Doreen's online course to become a Certified Angel Card Reader. I didn't really do much with that for some time. I was convinced that the teaching couldn't be effective online.

However, it gave me an important lesson, not just for card readings but for any career involving spirituality, and that is to trust your intuition. I also learned that everything is energy and if you trust and believe, spirit will guide you. It didn't matter if I was taught online or in person.

I continued to read Doreen Virtue's books and listen to her podcasts. I became familiar with Hay House Radio and several speakers and authors who specialized in spiritual and self-help teachings.

This is when I began listening to John Holland. Spirit was working its magic and I didn't even realize it.

CHAPTER TEN
My Life is Changing

John Holland is a Psychic Medium and I learned of his podcasts through Hay House Radio. He speaks not only about those who have crossed over but also about our spiritual journey. Both he and Doreen had a life-changing moment when they spiritually woke up. Doreen was the victim of a car-jacking and John was in a car accident. Mine was my sister's disappearance and death.

I went back to sleep for a few more years, but I didn't realize spirit was working behind the scenes. Work and family obligations were my way of avoiding the call on my life until I was ready.

In November 2011, I decided to go to Phoenix for a weekend retreat at the Celebrate Your Life Conference. I was guided to attend this conference and I trusted that feeling. I was eager to hear the amazing speakers that would be featured, including Doreen Virtue, John Holland, Wayne Dyer, and Dr. Andrew Weil. I not only enjoyed being with like-minded people but it felt like a huge weight was lifted off my shoulders.

Each individual speaking at this conference had a unique message on spirituality. All came from a place of love. What you give you will receive, so practicing your spirituality with love returns that love to you.

While at the conference, I attended John's session and

hoped to get a reading. I believe that Stephanie came through but it was by another reading for a couple whose son gave the message. The situations were similar and their ages were the same. I understood that his parents needed to hear this directly from John. I identified that this was also addressed to me from my sister.

I was impressed with John's abilities and when I returned home I visited his website to request his newsletter. He not only spoke to those who had crossed over but he also spoke about love, peace, forgiveness, and joy. This changed my way of thinking and I decided to re-read some of the books I had bought earlier. I realized that my perspective had changed for the better. I also became more aware of my spiritual gifts.

While on John's website one Monday afternoon, I read that John was going to appear in a new television program titled, "The UneXplained," on the BIO channel. They were asking people to submit their story with a chance to receive a reading from John that would be televised. The passing of the loved one had to be an unusual occurrence. Anyone interested must write a synopsis on the history of what happened and why they wanted a reading.

John would not be involved with this process because he didn't want to know too much prior to the reading. I submitted my letter and put my intention out into the Universe.

About four months later, I received a phone call.

"Is this Misty?" they asked.

I answered, "Yes, this is she."

The caller said, "I am a representative of the television series the UneXplained. We have read your story and found it very touching. We are interested in presenting it; however, John will not be doing your reading. Instead, the Psychic Twins will be involved with your storyline. We wanted to ask if you are still interested."

There was a lightness in my chest and I tried to contain my excitement when I answered, "Yes, of course I am still interested."

"We will be in touch with you soon. Do you have any questions?"

I had so many questions but didn't know where to begin.

I ended the conversation by saying, "I don't have questions now, but I am grateful that you are interested in our story. Thank you so much for helping us!"

After I hung up the phone, I called mom to tell her the news. Part of what I wrote in my letter was that I was hoping to give mom closure so she wouldn't have to live with her guilt any longer. I wasn't sure if this would do it, but I was willing to try.

I know that Stephanie had a hand in their choosing her story. I also knew without a doubt that she accepted the events of her life being made public. At the time of her disappearance, I felt she didn't want the details to come out. Stephanie was ashamed, embarrassed, and didn't want mom and dad to be hurt. Enough time had gone by that she was willing to have her story told.

I was excited that this was going to be nationally televised. Not only that, I was going to meet the Psychic Twins and was tremendously grateful for their involvement.

In March 2012, filming began at my house. The crew

was understanding and sensitive. It was tough reliving those memories. The production team was here for three days and on the second day I met the Psychic Twins.

They were awesome and throughout the day would give us mini readings. I could pick up on some feelings that I had about them and they would validate those thoughts. They said I was very intuitive and that I would write a book about my sister. That really bolstered my confidence.

The episode was titled, "Death in the Desert," and premiered on August 18, the day she disappeared 19 years earlier. This experience verified that Stephanie was with us and she is helping me now as I tell her story. The lessons I share from her life are not for her benefit, but for others who are in a destructive relationship or for family members who have lost someone to tragedy.

At this point I was closer to finding my purpose. In February 2014, I decided to go back to Celebrate Your Life in Scottsdale, Arizona. I had given Angel Card Readings to a co-worker who wanted to attend with me. Based on her cards, I felt certain that she was meant to attend. It was a great opportunity to be with like-minded people again and having a friend with me made it even better.

We were asked to choose our sessions in advance but there were so many it was difficult. We decided to go to separate talks and share what we heard.

I was drawn to two by Sunny Dawn Johnston. I knew of her teachings but had never heard her speak in person.

The date of the event was on my birthday. Throughout the weekend, I could feel my soul rising to a higher frequency.

When it was time for Sunny's courses, I could sense

her amazing energy. I was inspired by her journey to becoming a Psychic Medium and Angel Intuitive. She had a challenging beginning and I could relate to her story.

After that magical weekend, I was ready to discover my intended vocation. I still wasn't sure how I was going to manifest my gifts, but I did not need to know the why. Spirit had that part covered.

I still have a way to go, but I am on the right path. I believe God and his Angels are bringing opportunities to me. I operate from a place of love, not fear. It isn't always easy, but I strive to do my best.

In April of 2015, I retired from my Federal Law Enforcement job after 25 years. I decided to spend some time catching up on television and movies, enjoying my grandkids, and organizing the house. It was a time to rejuvenate and learn more about spirit. I vacationed in Southern California to see the ocean and cleanse any negativity I still carried.

In November of 2015, I learned that Sunny was offering a Mind, Body, and Spirit Practitioner Certification Course to be held in January 2016. I was led to sign up. I trusted that feeling and in January I went to Phoenix for a week to become a Certified Mind, Body, and Spirit Practitioner. I was able to take in Sunny's positive energy.

The training was intense but the atmosphere was electrifying. The participants were spirit-centered seekers of truth. We studied several topics including the need to be confident in our abilities. Sounds simple, but it wasn't. Being in the company of these women was empowering. We all had different needs, but Sunny tailored every subject to our individual gifts.

None of us wanted the week to end but I was so proud when I completed the course. I had learned so much, and my purpose became clear. I knew going back into the real world was going to be difficult, but I remembered what I had been taught: Trust your intuition, and approach each situation from a place of love. If I face a challenging situation, I call on my Guardian Angel and Spirit Guides to help me.

Attending her course gave me the courage to take my next step and accept my calling. When I returned home I started my spiritual-based business. I asked our local Small Business Development Center for their assistance. I live in a small town and people shy away from talk about the spirit world even though they do believe.

I trust in what I am given, and believe I am guided by spirit to help people manifest their destiny. My business is growing and people are discovering their purpose, and thanking me for offering these opportunities in our town.

As I lay in bed in January 2016, I felt someone push down on my bed as if they were trying to slip their arm under me to give me a hug. I felt a tingling sensation up and down my body and opened my eyes, but saw no one. At that moment, a voice said, 'It is time to start writing your book about Stephanie and it will be titled, By Your Side, because your sister, your angels and your spirit guides are always with you.'

A few days later, Sunny shared a post on Facebook about a writing intensive to help people write their book. Spirit was speaking and I followed the guidance. I am blessed to have so many beautiful spirits in this realm and the next by my side.

EPILOGUE
By Your Side

Stephanie and I were destined to be together. We both picked the same parents; however, we picked very different lives. Most people with sisters and brothers will have some sibling rivalry, and can relate to the volatile relationship Stephanie and I had. We loved each other, were jealous of each other, but sometimes we almost hated each other.

I believe our souls were meant to have those feelings in the physical world, so we could better appreciate each other in the spiritual world.

Since her transition in August of 1993, she has been with me in spirit. She needed my forgiveness on her spiritual journey. That is why she came to me when she was missing. She knew that I would put aside our differences and give her my unconditional love.

I am grateful that she sought my guidance and asked me to tell her story. It is also clear to me that because she deeply hurt me in the physical world, she had to make amends in the spiritual realm.

When she spoke to me, I realized I could communicate with those who have passed, and she has been with me ever since.

Today, I provide Angel Card Readings, Spiritual Guidance, and workshops on Angels. The pieces in the puzzle of my life are falling into place, and the loss and sorrow of my sister's death were part of my destiny.

I thank Stephanie for guiding me, and although she left this world at a young age, her spirit is still present. I can hear her now saying, "Don't worry, I'll always be by your side."

MEMORIES

Figure 1: Misty and Stephanie - 1970

Figure 2: Misty and Stephanie - 1971

Figure 3: Misty and Stephanie - 1973

Figure 4: Stephanie – 1973

Figure 5: Misty and Stephanie - 1974

Figure 6: Misty, Granny & Stephanie - 1975

Figure 7: Misty, Mom and Stephanie - 1975

Figure 8: Stephanie, Mom and Misty - 1975

Figure 9: Stephanie - 1984

Figure 10: Mom and Stephanie - 1984

Figure 11: Family Photo - 2016

ABOUT THE AUTHOR

Misty is a best-selling author, psychic medium, angel intuitive, space clearer, and speaker. In 2016, she created her business, Mystified Enlightenment and has since helped many people on their life path utilizing her abilities as an Angelic Life Coach, Certified Angel Card Reader, and Mind, Body, & Spirit Practitioner. She is married, has four children, four grandchildren, and four step-grandchildren and lives in Thatcher, Arizona. She enjoys writing and traveling to the beach. Her first published book, "The Peacemakers: Restoring Love in the World through Stories of Compassion and Wisdom" was a best-selling book on Amazon. Misty wrote about restoring self-love in oneself before peace in the world can be restored. In Misty's second book, "The Best of Spiritual Writers Network 2016", she writes about her experience in Sedona, Arizona. This book was another best-selling book at Amazon and she was a contest winner chosen among hundreds of submissions.

Misty has two more compilation books that will soon be published, "Top Picks, Spiritual Leaders: Stories of Wisdom, Inspiration, and Healing" where she discusses judgements and how we can turn that into light. Her next submission is entitled, "365 Days of Angel Prayers Book", where Misty has submitted an angel prayer about gratitude.

All her book submissions have prepared her for "By Your Side". This has been a tremendous healing experience for her and she hopes that others who have experienced a tragic death of a loved one will be able to relate to the pain, guilt, and remorse one has had and the spiritual healing one can encounter.

Misty enjoys working with her clients and can channel loved ones who has passed along with the angelic realm to help them with their life lessons and to be the best version of themselves. This is her true life's purpose and receives a great amount of joy helping others.

Contact Information:

Email: contact@mistymthompson.com

Facebook:
www.facebook.com/mystifiedenlightenment.com

Website: www.mistymthompson.com

CPSIA information can be obtained
at www.ICGtesting.com
Printed in the USA
LVOW10s2236190417
531424LV00005B/32/P

9 780998 757667